Small Wants Little Needs

The Spiritual and Practical Solution To Becoming Financially Free

By Ian Fox

Copyright and Special Note:

ISBN: 978-1-4710-9895-6

Dedication:

To all those who are sick of the rat-race, the lies, illusions and tricks and wish to live spiritually and financially free now.

Contents:

Dedication:

Foreword:

Chapter 1:   **Why I Wrote This Book**

Chapter 2:   **The Ball And Chain**

Chapter 3:   **The Art of Having Less**

Chapter 4:   **Don't Work For Money - Work To Be Free**

Chapter 5:   **Work For Less Time**

Chapter 6:   **Work For More Money**

Chapter 7:   **You Only Want What You Observe**

Chapter 8:   **Stand Guard At The Door Of Your Mind**

Chapter 9:   **Be Still, Be Silent**

Chapter 10:   **Let Go And Grow**

Chapter 11:   **Master Your Own Conscious-Reality**

Chapter 12:   **Your Financial Freedom Plan**

Chapter 13:   **Everything Comes To Those Who..?**

Chapter 14:   **Bring More Lightness To Your Life**

Chapter 15: **The Fear Solution**

Chapter 16: **Mission Freedom**

About the Author:

*The perfect man (or woman) employs
his/her mind as a mirror. It grasps
nothing; it refuses nothing. It receives, but
it does not keep*

Zen Saying

Foreword:

They say loving money is the root of all evil, but lacking it forces you to put out the wrong energy. To me, ego and unconsciousness is the root of all evil. In our culture you need money to avoid being trapped in scarcity and negative obligation, but the greatest danger with money is being driven by materialism, object addiction and greed. If you have debts on the things you own, then you are to a greater or lesser degree trapped by the very things you once thought would release you or make you happy. Even if they have no financial commitment you may still have to think about or maintain them.

This book is about changing your perceptions of money and aligning to the most incredibly powerful resource you have, which is raising your consciousness and awareness around money, ego and materialistic value.

In a way, you are shaken awake from the trance of endless yearning and feeling as though you are not good enough. A release from the insatiable appetite of wanting more and never feeling truly satisfied. The constant illusion of happiness through things leads to object emptiness, which is broken and replaced with dynamic balance, pure control and personal freedom. Not only will you break free on a spiritual level but also on the level of financial freedom. The money you do earn is not used to feed your ego, because you will have transcended it by then, but to create a perfect living experience based on release, choice and ego-free joy.

There is no doubt that times are challenging and the world will have to untangle the mess the collective unconscious has created. Rich bankers, politicians and bureaucrats have made a total mess of things and as usual the people have to pay the price. If the people awaken from their trance, which is being forced, and transcend the ego's grip, the power exalted on the public by the governments, institutions and greedy marketers will be neutralised.

Unless you have enough money you'll struggle to be free and be shackled to the background noise of obligation to debts and negative circumstances. You can be free mentally, psychologically and financially, but you have to wake up and take action. Not only that but you need to create a plan which will deliver the money and set you free. This book will help you do that.

It is our god-given right to be free and abundant, but our mounting consumer led society has become increasingly more difficult to satisfy. When you live in a constant state of feeling as though you do not have enough or are good enough, you are trapped, and at the mercy of commercial influence and susceptible to unconscious acceptance. There is abundance everywhere you look, but it is not necessarily about being rich and flashing the cash!

It's having more than enough money so you have no debt, no financial stress or worry and live very comfortably, having the freedom to choose what you want to do. You don't have to maintain a BS charade or be hooked on wanting acceptance and approval from people. What you create money for, what you spend it on, and what you think about money comes out of a higher state of consciousness not ego.

Many people are unaware when it comes to their ego and perception of money; they just feel as though they are desperate to have it and total failures if they don't. Many use money as a way to prove their status and feel as though they are more attractive, and to some unconscious members' of the opposite sex they temporarily can be. Some use it to mask inadequacies, fears and issues. Others to make a difference to people.

But these things seldom last and sooner or later will ultimately create suffering. The only answer to being free is to raise your spiritual consciousness, be debt free and have enough money to meet all your needs. This may take time if your current life situation is far from serene. But you have to start now not later. This book is not about debt planning or management but teaches you about overcoming your ego and the psychology of money, as well as offering you some practical and useful tools to help you on your journey. Learning about and mastering your ego is one of the most powerful of all spiritual lessons in life, because until you do, you remain in pain and trapped.

Most people are unconscious of their own ego and how controlled they are by it. But once you become more aware you trigger a chain reaction of taking responsibility for your life and circumstances. Being *response-able* for your life and who and what influences you, gives your power back to you. Once you elevate your consciousness you create an easier life for yourself and those you care about. You see, most people are facing a serious financial crisis, unless they change.

With all the government "spending-cuts," unemployment rises, tax increases and mounting cost of living. People's incomes are squeezed more than ever! Most household incomes are severely under-funded when it comes to managing their money and even worse, once their careers wind down they have little to fall back on. You can forget your pension and winning the lottery.

However, those who get focused, get conscious and control their ego's, will potentially sidestep any economic quicksand, vastly increase their income and enhance their living standards. With all the economic uncertainty and global instability around it can be easy to get drawn into 'poverty consciousness.' Today we are surrounded by 'doom and gloom' merchants and susceptible to the toxic fallout of well-meaning friends and family.

Our parents and grandparents were conditioned to believe you had to work hard and slave your guts out to get anywhere in life. "Life is hard and struggle honourable." They usually handed this down to their children, who then passed it on to theirs and so on. The antithesis of this is getting rich and famous quickly with a glamorous career, appearing on a reality TV show, becoming a footballer or marrying one!

With multi-millionaire pop-stars and reality show contestants supposedly raking it in, it can be very alluring to the ego to choose that route to find fulfilment. But of course we know that is a total BS illusion and quickly brings out the opposite of what it was supposed to deliver. History is full of examples and warnings of people who have chased glamour, fame and excessive riches only to discover it brought them pain and suffering in the end.

Finding the happy balance and having your monetary needs met (or surpassed) is key. Not chasing the illusion or fantasy that money, status and things will fulfil you. Stagnation is a prison and the status-quo a trap. For things to change you actually need to DO something – take ACTION! Most of the time people get caught up in the trap of earning a living instead of being the architect of their future. They become slaves to the system and in turn time passes and they remain stuck in the layer cake of life. I'm sure you want to take control of your own destiny and not want to rely on corrupt governments and controlling legislation.

If you've thought about stepping away from the rat-race, cutting your dependence on credit and wish to be free then this book is going to give you the inspiration and practical advice you need to make the lifestyle "move" you've been looking for. Forget all the commuting or scraping the ice off the car on a frosty Monday morning, boss breathing down your neck, assholes up your nose - that's for other people - not you!

I assume you're not the sort of person to rely on "Luck" or *winning money,* but want to control your own destiny rather than being at the mercy of the economy or the financial markets. The world is full of "survivors," those who just make it by. Living from pay-check to pay-check and month to month, one payday short of total financial collapse.

Believe me, you don't want to be in debt and broke in the coming years - it will be a major drag. You are responsible for making things happen. If you do not start to take action, you will be left behind I'm sorry to have to say! It's time to snap out of the trance and do something that can take your life into a better, more fulfilling and spiritually transformational direction.

There has never been a better time for you to be reading this book because it can be the catalyst which sets you free. It's time for your awakening.

Come on let's go...

Be not afraid of growing slowly; be afraid
only of standing still
Chinese Proverb

Chapter 1:

Why I Wrote This Book

I remember losing my temper for some really trivial reason, being uncharacteristically snappy, together with an unsettling increase in heart palpitations. Getting colds almost every other week and constantly experiencing low energy and lethargy. I'm ashamed to admit, I could even be found checking my email late on Christmas Eve and even when relaxing, not completely switch-off. When moving house, the day the removal men arrived, I was still on my PC! Making sure it was the last thing to be disconnected. Almost every conversation was work related. I would read books whilst watching TV, listen to audios in the shower and even on holiday packed the suitcase with more books/audios than clothes (apart from my ego caressing brands and Ray-Bans).

I attended almost every business and motivational seminar going. I was like a Tasmanian devil; my life became a 'doing-filled' whirlwind. I just never stopped. Looking back it was crazy, just crazy. I had the expected fancy cars, country house and decorated my life with designer brands. I was into my image, look and tight t-shirts. Despite having the symbols of success and trinkets of accomplishments, I still felt empty and dissatisfied inside. Hollow and superficial. My life seemed to be nothing more than a cycle of paying debts and taxes, punctuated with the occasional fleeting pleasure and retail or motor-trade fix. I would regularly ask myself *"is this all there is?"*

I guess you could say I was working crazy-hard because I was being unconsciously driven to avoid the painful memories of my childhood. I was one of 10 children growing up in a council house in Crich, Derbyshire. We had very little money and my father was a freaky disciplinarian who looked after us all when my mother fell ill with MS (Multiple Sclerosis). We lived off dripping (fat and juices from roasted meat), breakfast cereal with watered down milk and tripe (the yucky stomach lining of animals).

I remember the horrible feeling of going to bed hungry almost every night and when bucked up enough courage, daringly sneaking downstairs to steal biscuits for my sisters and me. If I was caught my father would have beaten me into obedience with the buckle of his belt as he'd done to my brothers. But I didn't have to worry about that, because shortly afterwards a padlock appeared on the cupboard door containing the biscuits. Despite that, he would still count the number of biscuits left in the packet each day.

The other idea I had was to store food in my bedroom, so I would create a stash of rations in the back of the drawer. This worked until I ate the eggs I'd been hiding, giving me an almost fatal dose of salmonella food poisoning. I never really had the proper medical treatment and ceremoniously collapsed on the toilet. I lost 2 stone (28 pounds) in 12 days. My sisters really thought I was done for and for a while, so did I. I had many visions of light and angels whilst unconscious, and silhouettes of shadowy human figures holding hands, although I couldn't make any sense of it at the time and rarely talked about it.

Now I understand. I asked God, why was I suffering? But then realised this was the only time I'd ever asked God anything! In that moment I had a deep sense of inner peace. I realised the presence of God in your heart eclipses all suffering.

I vowed when I grew up, would never go hungry (or eat raw-eggs) and would have abundance in my life. The problem of course is when the pendulum of destiny swings the other way and you then become a slave to the potential for pain and avoidance of your unconscious memories. In a way you forget some of life's greatest lessons by getting caught up in the daily rituals of western society:

Get a job or career, earn money, buy things, earn more money, buy more things, get a house, then get a bigger house, consume, conquer, compete, buy even more things, show-off, prove yourself, be accepted, yearn for more, push, shove, struggle, fight, peruse, judge, resent, consume even more, waste increase, waist increase, health decrease, mind disease, frustration, life dissatisfaction, consume more and more, still frustrated, still spiritually constipated, trapped behind the prison bars of success, achievement and the illusion that money is a God. Grow old, get fat, waste life and die!

Mostly the entire western world is caught up in the trap of materialism, ego and glamour obsession. People work hard to try to sustain the illusion of success and achievement only to remain unfulfilled, superficial and empty. There is a shift happening in the world albeit by default, people are no longer willing to tolerate working themselves into an early grave or existing in what I call a "living death." Which is virtually the same as waking dead! There is more to life than slaving away at a job you hate, a boss you can't stand and trading your time for money just to keep the wheels spinning.

Our society is full of stressed out workaholics who's ego have their balls so tight they can hardly walk and schedules so crammed there's hardly time to take a pee!

With all the social networking to complete, the things to do and the obligations to meet, the stresses and struggles of life can manifest in a plethora of negative expressions. I have nothing against social networking, it has its place. The problem is when it becomes obsessive and compulsive. For many it's a modern form of *ego-massaging*. A friend once said "I've no time for business; I'm too busy social networking."

This book is not about debt management or spending plans, although, if you're in-debt then some financial management and action is required. Ultimately its purpose is to set you free from the destiny of the masses, which is slavery to 'tick-tock.' This can only happen when you become more aware of how our culture can trap you into a never ending cycle of work-debt-obligation. This book will teach you how to play and win at the money game and help you liberate yourself from the bondage of control, manipulation by the corporations and the traps of egoic possession.

I know what it's like to work yourself half to death. I've climbed the ladder of success, put in ridiculous hours (all the while, kept telling myself it's temporary) concentrated to the point where my brain hurts. As I said, I played hard to maintain a lifestyle, a social position and meet my ego's demands. I've done that part, I've got the t-shirt! I learned that life was never meant to be a hard labour prison sentence. There are easier, simpler and more rewarding ways to pay the bills and live your life. I created a system for living financially free, meeting all your needs and breaking free of the intensity of the ego's grip.

BEING RICH DOES NOT MEAN BEING FREE

You see unless you transcend your ego you will be imprisoned forever and never be truly free. I realise whatever you want to do in life takes money and the ultimate leverage of money is having more time, more choice. There is a price for freedom. That's why I can't understand these so-called millionaires who seem to be busier than ever and more trapped by their ego's than they would like to admit. To me money is about freedom, not just being rich, it's having the time to authentically and wholly enjoy it.

The problem is most rich people are scared of losing their "competitive edge," disappearing into obscurity and letting go. They have a lot of ego wrapped up inside their career identity. Their live story! They have illusionary positions to defend and status symbols to symbolically polish.

You don't own anything anyway and everything you have is temporary and part of the 'one-energy' on loan from a higher power. Most people in our society are trapped on the giant mouse wheel of life, estranged from the true essence of who they are beyond their job, status and belongings. They are wrapped up in form.

That's what this book is all about... setting you free from the drudgery, illusion and pain. I want to teach you the system I created and personally use inside this book.

Chapter 2:

The Ball And Chain

Most of what we think is real, is an illusion. We are conditioned from a very early age to place a high value on materialism, form, designer brands, cars, glamour, gadgets and gizmos. In our society the value of success is measured on how much you consume and what you have. Money is a symbol of success, but it means little unless it brings you freedom. Money is neutral but you can't be free without it and living in a cardboard box is not everyone's cup of tea! Money should buy choice, time and peace of mind. Debt on the other hand is entrapment, negative obligation imbued with emotional weight.

There is nothing wrong in wanting better things in your life or having the trappings of success. As long as you are not paying for it long after the shine has worn off or you are feeding the ego by showing off and seeking admirers. You have to be brutally honest with yourself sometimes and be aware of why you make the choices and decisions you make. Short lived ego satisfaction is a disease of the mind. You can only tame it with awareness, discipline and practicing delayed gratification.

The problem with owning things is that they tend to own you. You have to think about them, tend to them, worry about them, have to pay for them. Take an expensive car for example. You have to watch where you park. Wonder if anyone is going to scratch it? Clean it, insure it, and more than likely have to meet the monthly payment on it? It saps your energy and is another obligation that keeps you enslaved to the system. The other –

illusion is the "object" somehow elevates your social status and class. Things can never help you raise your energy; they can only mask the feeling of inadequacy. Conforming to the expectations of social groups, peers and family will never fulfil you long term. You will only feel free when the pressure to be someone subsides and is replaced with a feeling of oneness and serenity with all things.

Most people are held hostage by their ego, striving to fulfil its demands, having to have this or that, the best car, live in the best house, wear the best clothes, seeking admirers and approval from others. I can understand the ancient aspect of trying to become pack leader and find a mate, but this does not fill the void. This just leads to further pain because like I said, what you own ultimately ends up owning you. It's not that you should have the complete opposite of these things; you must control the ego with discipline, the discipline of a spiritual awakening. If you lack restraint the ego will just keep dragging you down.

The ego promises to set you free once you meet its temporary demands, but then it hits you with a new list of desires. Believe me; you will never be free or happy if you do not control it. Some egomaniacs get defensive when they hear suggestions of taming the ego with discipline; they declare they would starve without its rule. This might be the case, but they are not free, they live the bondage of the ego. These characters get highly stressed; feel immense pressure to perform and their worldly possessions contain a psychological weight that consumes all their 'spiritual' powers. It's amazing how the more you seem to have the more empty you feel.

WHAT YOU OWN, OWNS YOU!

Simplifying your life and getting back to the spirit within you is the only way to truly find peace in this chaotic world. You will never be free until you don't owe anything and have little weight holding you down. At least this is a major part of your quest to live an unrestricted life, without being shackled to the system.

The main problem is if your life is so crammed full of activity, such as intellectualising things, paying bills/debts, owning objects or trying to keep up with your social media, etc, you will never be free. You need to simplify your life and trim your mind of extraneous thoughts. Less mess is less stress.

THE FREEDOM QUESTION

When you awake to a new day what are the questions you ask? Is there any tension or contraction in your mind and body about the new day ahead? Freedom is always about, not what you have to do, but what you "choose" to do. For many that question is far from their consciousness as they jump or should I say fall out of bed only to connect to the mainframe of human slavery and egoic entrapment.

"I have to go to work to pay my bills" is the mantra that most of society lives by and on a practical level this is the case. As long as you do not misinterpret the word 'practical?' Freedom is about having very few bills other than the essentials. This does not mean living a pauper's life or living on pennies per day just so that you can be 'Bill Free.' If your bills are feeding your ego (now or in the past), giving you status elevation, or bringing suffering to yourself and others then this is another trap you –

have fallen into. Money, which is nothing more than a form of energy, should come from something you love to do that raises the lives of other people and not from the "me" "mine" or collection of things. It should also be low maintenance and not require vast amounts of time or thinking, although it may require large investments of both initially?

You may say, "there is nothing I can do about my situation at the moment." This may be the case, but there are things you can do. You can accept where you are. This does not mean giving up and staying stuck. As much as if you fell over and was covered in mud from head to toe, would you never wash again? You would change your clothes, shower and keep your eyes open next time.

Fully accept this moment without hesitation or reservation because your resistance to it brings you more pain. All things take time. You may say that you cannot accept the way things are? Then accept the fact that you cannot accept. This in itself can be very transforming. You can also bring a sense of enjoyment to your doing.

It is the human frailty to get lost in doing and forget about being. You may say you do not enjoy what you are doing? This is because you are forgetting about being.

If you do not enjoy what you are doing then you can only ever do one of two things?

1: Change it. 2: Accept it

The freedom morning question is *"what do I want to do today"* and not "what do I have to do today." It may take time to reach the point in your life when you can ask that question from a level of higher awareness and mean it. Not from the ego. Ego is doing, awareness is being.

Power Tip:

1. Accept this moment whatever shape it takes
2. Trim your life, less mess is less stress
3. See money as energy, nothing more

Fox Freedom Factor Maxim:

You can only be free to the degree to which you are not trapped by physical, financial or mental obligation

Chapter 3:

The Art of Having Less

Unless you overcome the vice like grip of the ego, you will never be free, and unless you raise your awareness and consciousness you will be trapped for life.

We live in a culture that reveres having possessions and status. The major marketing companies and institutions know this and want to control the people with debt, materialism and object obsession. There is nothing wrong in wanting to better your circumstances and improve the lives of your family. The problem is when you define who you are by what you have and compare what you have with what others have. Craving for things that go beyond your survival, just to feed the ego and satisfy the perception you think the world has of you. It's all designed to keep you trapped, small and un-evolved.

By having/wanting less you will save yourself from the pain and anguish that most humans endure day after day as they crave for more and identify with material form. Many people only exist on the physical level and rarely connect with their inner or higher self, they remain prisoners of their own egos as they fight to maintain the demands of today's society along with the majority of other humans.

Living in an ashram is not for everyone and you may have to hold down a job, raise the kids and balance your life. This is true, but there are easier more effective ways of achieving balance and tranquillity. At a core level the essence of who you are is a free spirit. Life was not meant to be a constant struggle from one drama/situation to another. Materials and ego gratification seem to offer temporary rest bite from the challenges modern life brings, but they are fleeting and more often than not have a higher price to pay.

Once you go from ego to flow you raise your energy and feel the power of the enlightened soul which is not shackled to objects, material form, opinions and endless yearning.

DO NOT BECOME THE BASTARD LOVE CHILD OF GLAMOUR AND MONEY

Did that statement get your attention? I thought so, but please understand it is not my intention to insult you, instead I want your attention. *Sometimes we all need to be shaken to awaken from our trance.* We live in a world where money is a god and glamour its lover. Where you slave your life away to pay your debts and give your ego another fix. The result is continual dissatisfaction and suffering. To live your life in a constant state of disquiet and disappointment is a heck of a waste. This is why, on the positive side, millions of people turn to Meditation, T'ai Chi and Yoga, etc and on the negative side, find solace in drink, drugs, over eating, gambling and loveless sex, etc. They look for a way out of pain.

The problem is although these activities help mask the pain, they only provide temporary relief. You can only grow and increase your life-force when you raise your consciousness. This can only begin once you tame the ego and control compulsive thinking.

It would be true to say, most people do not know who they really are and only identify themselves by what they own, their status, credentials, etc. They believe, "I live in a big house, drive a nice car, and have lovely clothes, so that makes me who I am?" They define themselves based upon how much they have achieved and collected in this world. It is very interesting that many "glamorous" stars turn to drugs, drink or withdraw further into a void between so-called normal and abnormal. Rehab is the buzz word of show business. This is because they realise, what they own and what people think of them is not who they really are. The inner person recognises it.

The ego is very much attached to things and hates change or contradictions. This is why you should practice being spontaneous and making a conscious effort to deny gratification and short lived pleasures to confuse the ego. To keep the ego in check try this, if you feel like dessert, don't have it. If you feel like sex, abstain. Keep the old car and those clothes are ok. Make this your practice from time to time. The more you do this, the more you *will like it*. Trust me.

The problem is the human mind is caught up in the virus of thought, which can be all consuming and controlling. Incessant mental chatter, judgement and labelling leads to imbalance and will certainly dilute and pollute the energy of your life-force. Your ultimate goal is to settle the waves of the turbulent mind and enable yourself to recognise you are more than what you own and have.

All pain and suffering is the result of the ego, judging, labelling and contradictions to your expectations. The ego left unchecked, will leave you empty, alone and afraid. Forget your fancy car, designer jeans and smart phone. They only mask what you are truly looking for inside and you will always feel empty if this is all you have.

Personally I would rather be a bum living on the street than be someone's slave. Towed around by the nose, like an animal, by some dunderhead who did not have my highest interests at heart. It wouldn't bother me because I know that my higher self, God, Supreme Being, Mother Superior or whatever name you want to give it would look after me. I would resonate at a higher frequency than your average street occupant. Opportunities and the right circumstances would show up and align to the energy I was putting out. Remember, whilst you resist your circumstances, they persist.

HATING YOUR CREDIT RATING

I used to worry about my credit rating. I used be obsessed with protecting it, until I realised if you need credit, then you really can't afford it. You might say "but I can't go out and buy a house without credit and for that I need a good credit score, more than ever these days." You need to ask, *who has conditioned you to believe that?*

Did you know that mortgage means *until death*? Mort is a French word meaning "*death*" and gage means "pledge or *agreement.*" As you can see the real meaning of the word mortgage is "*agreement till death.*" Very inspiring isn't it! Imagine if when you trundled off to the Bank and said to the manager, you were there to see him about the death agreement!!

25

If you do get a Mortgage, then get *the best deal you can for the lowest cost and duration you can.* It's a roof over your head at the end of the day. If you want to live in a big house to impress people, then it's you who will *pay* the ultimate price. Who wants to live at 42 Egocentric Cul-de-sac!

The institutions want to keep you trapped (*sealed*) in debt and obligation, because this is how *they* control you. That is what they want; *you locked in forever or for as long as possible.* You need to seek liberation and educate yourself out of the collective unconsciousness of the masses. Life is a pyramid; you see there are those at the top of the pyramid and those at or near the bottom. These are the slaves helping to keep the entire thing going.

Living a simpler way of life - not *owing* or *owning* so much is my way. The truth is, today's treasures become tomorrow's trash. For most part anyway, the ego needs things now, it won't wait for you to save up, and this induces many to get into debt, which only adds more weight and more strain to their lives.

Most people get caught up in the traps of the ego, slip into a trance, and are then forced to carry the burden. I remember buying a car on credit, the sparkle, the newness, the thought of what others might think of me, my ego really had me by the proverbials! Driving it away from the dealership with the cheesy grin of the salesman waving me on, my ego really felt great! It didn't take long before the freshness wore off; it got dirty, and left me with a four year heavyweight monthly obligation and a gargantuan interest payment.

The ego in its desires to be fulfilled misses the finite details, the small print if you like. When do we want it? *Our ego's want it now, not later.* When we succumb to its pressure, there is a hefty price to pay – I call it *"Outcome Tax."* Either way you look at it, there is a toll to pay for the material things you want.

Once you disconnect with your ego you begin to unleash an inner guide, a new (or old) powerful you. You are no longer at the mercy of its demands, you become free. Equally you live with power, fortitude and have an air about you which resonates on a much higher frequency than that of the tribe. You don't have to show off or seek admirers – you have a silent strength which omits from your very core.

Have you ever met a person who didn't say that much, you just knew they had something different about them? They were not seeking admirers or a *"look-at-me"* personality. They were almost invisible except you noticed or were drawn to them. They walked and moved with presence. They didn't get involved in pointless banter or idle conversation, rather when they spoke; they did so with reverence and uncommon wisdom. Most people only experience life on a physical/exterior level. They only see what they have from the point of the ego. They identify with the objects they have around them, what they own, and what others think of them. You don't really own anything and you can't take it with you. Unconsciousness in most people is deeply engrained, conditioned and rooted.

It's very difficult to escape the pull of the ego unless you become more conscious. You can budget, abstain, delay, refuse and say "No" as much as you like, but the only way out of dysfunction is to raise your consciousness of the formless.

Luckily if you apply what you read in this book, a brighter light will shine upon your path.

Power Tip:

1. Live a simpler way of life
2. Tame the ego with discipline and control compulsive thinking by raising your awareness of what is on your mind
3. Look beyond the veil of materialism

Fox Freedom Factor Maxim:

Don't derive your identity from what you consume and own

Chapter 4:

Don't Work For Money – Work To Be Free

A university professor visited Nan-in to enquire about Zen. Nan-in served tea. He filled the professor's cup and then kept on pouring. The professor watched the overflow until he could restrain himself no longer. 'It is overfull - No more will go in.' 'like this cup,' Nan-in said, 'you are full of your own opinions and speculations. How can I show you Zen unless you first empty your cup?'

That's the problem with most people... they over think or suffer from what I call *"Thought-itis!"* This is an inflammation of the over-anal gland, most commonly caused by an inflated ego. Symptoms of *"Thought-itis"* include wanting to know everybody's business and a mild to severe sense of insignificance. Which, the sufferer tries to overcome with short-lived egoic gratification.

Through the process of this book, you will discover by slowing the mind, controlling the ego and simplifying your life, your thoughts will eventually become calmer, more powerful, and sustainable. This gives rise to *YOUR* real *'inner power'* being released. You'll eventually realise you don't need all that stuff anymore to feel significant. The majesty, beauty and all-knowing essence of you will begin to appear. In my view, the only reason to work is to be free and not just for the money.

I agree, there are other values obtained through your vocation and if you are meeting your passion (not just satisfying the ego), then perhaps you are already somewhat liberated?

Money is all about security and feeling safe. Often a job or career gives you the illusion you have both. For the most part it's just a trap you have quietly fallen into. You get conditioned to having a salary and trotting off to work. There is nothing wrong with having a job by the way. If it gets you out of the house and meeting people and makes you happy, then all well and good. However, for most this is certainly not the case.

DO NOT BE A SHEEPLE!

This book is about freedom and nonconformity. If you are content with where you are and what you have (not in the "*thing*" sense) then "tickety-boo!" I wrote this book because others have admired and commented on my way of life and how I live. This formed the desire in me to help others escape the mouse-wheel, rat-race, treadmill, *prison without bars*, or by any other name? Help them discover omnipresent balance and a higher purpose beyond everyday "sheeple-living-activity."

If like me, you wanted to break free from the rhythms of social conditioning, a stereotyped lifestyle and the illusion which says you have to work until you're too old, then this book is your portal. I'm sure there is a voice inside you resonating with that at some level. Isn't that the reason why you are reading this book? Your work or what you do to earn money should contribute to your freedom, not compound the entrapment. If you have a big mortgage, masses of debt and endless commitments, you're stuck, entangled in the tapestry of negative obligation and interest payments.

The first thing you must do is workout a plan to pay off your debts. If you are in prison you have two choices. *1: Wait for your sentence to end or 2: Start digging a tunnel.* It's no use looking to run away from where you are right now. If you owe a lot of money then you may have to put out extra energy and effort to earn enough to payoff what is owed. It's like losing weight, a person doesn't get fat quickly, the extra pounds accumulate over time, until one day a gigantic 'kick up the consciousness' comes along such as a health risk, and calories start getting counted.

The primary reason debts escalate is because one assumes the future is going to be better than the present in financial terms. You have to create a plan, take action, get focussed and make things happen. Starting now!

WEALTH IS ALWAYS RELATIVE

When you are in a better position financially, you can concentrate on earning money to help set you free and not just to pay your debts. If you still have debts, they will be easy to manage and over the shortest payment term possible. Wealth is always relative to what you bring in compared to what you pay out. If you payout more than you bring in then you are perpetually trapped. Again, this book is not about debt management. There are plenty of books on the subject, covering payment plans, snowball systems, amortisation tactics, etc. I will give you some methods on creating wealth and income inside this book, without you working yourself half to death in the drudgery of the *collective sheeple*. First you have to face your financial reality and wake up from the trance of credit.

It's a fallacy that money brings security. Yes, money may help you deal with your dysfunction more comfortably, but the ego of the masses is firmly shackled to the illusion which says, you are more secure because you have more money in the bank and own more stuff. I know many millionaires who are totally insecure and psychologically phobic. Even some of the world's most "rich and famous" are deeply unhappy and totally insecure, beyond the charade of glamour and their public face. Their wealth can bring out the nasty side of their personality and frequently reinforces one giant ego-trip. They become neurotic and worry about their status and wealth being taken away from them. In reality they may be recognised by the masses, but they are neither free nor happy. This dark cloud obscures the happiness they thought the fame and money would bring them. Many celebrities now hate their fame.

FAME IS AN ILLUSION OF SMOKE AND MIRRORS

Money is only worth anything when it transports you across the chasm from anxiety to freedom and brings inner peace. I once thought I wanted to be famous, travelling the world doing my one-man contortion show. I got to know many famous people and after seeing the reality from the inside, I can tell you the inane ugliness changed my mind. Many a celebrity told me on the quiet, they would give anything to go back to obscurity. I would respond: *"Once the toothpaste is out the tube you can't put it back in!"*

Having more money is not always the answer to your sensed problems. Many are deluded into thinking the more money they make, the more secure and happier they'll feel. This is why so many fall under the spell of the "millionaire get rich quick schemes?"

If you are out of balance with the money you do make, then making more will only magnify your dysfunction. If you are feeding your ego with objects and credit, spending more than you make, then financial equilibrium is the problem.

This is why controlling the ego is the only way out of financial turmoil and pain. You must take back control with discipline and mental strength and have the courage to recognise your circumstances for what they are, and take action to bring about a return to balance. Don't be worried about what people will think, because this is yet another ego-trap. If people say "what happened to the car?" you reply *"I am practising a spot of material pruning and bringing more lightness to my life."* That will break their pattern for sure! You wouldn't believe the feeling of lightness you'll feel, when you remove the crud and crap from your life.

Do you give yourself a hard time if you can't afford to buy new things now? This is because you are not content where you are and think the future with this item in your life will make you feel better than your current circumstances allow. This is all part of the misinterpretation of an egoic motive, which clouds the mind, getting in the way of finding inner peace and joy without relying on circumstances to meet your expectations.

What you need to remember is every experience is imbued with the seed of wisdom. The problem for the most part being, you can't yet see it. When you stop and think about it, from the egoic false illusionary standard on which success is judged, Mother Teresa would be considered a failure. I doubt she had a big bank balance, no fancy car, plush office or need for brand labels. But, I'm sure at the end of life, she left richly rewarded for all the goodness she had created, not for the objects she had collected.

33

The reason why many experience immense instability in life is because they carry too much weight in terms of obligation, debt, and they are at the mercy of their ego. They carry this negative energy around like an overloaded suitcase trolley at the airport. Adopt the discipline of never allowing a situation, thing or person to inherently control you. Do not buy into the emotions, but seek resolutions. Ask yourself "*do I really need this or will it trap me?*" Always think before you act and maintain a spiritual balance and serenity around money and material objects.

MUCH OF WHAT YOU EARN IS NOT YOURS TO KEEP

See your work, other than the personal fulfilment it gives you, as a means towards your freedom from the ritual of routine and repetitive obligation. Look at earning as a way of learning about yourself and realise your time in your current earthly body is short and temporary. Why waste it slaving away working for your creditors or paying heaps of taxes, etc? Look for the solution and your way out, because there is one. See money as a stepping stone, not the goal and work to free yourself.

Power Tip:

1. Work to free yourself from obligation and debt
2. Think before you act about money and credit
3. Don't allow people or situations to control you

Fox Freedom Factor Maxim:

The feeling of financial and spiritual lightness is always better than the weight of being materially rich

Chapter 5:

Work For Less Time

There is a lot written about working shorter hours a day and even as little as a few hours a week, but for most people this is a complete fallacy. They simply don't have the infrastructure and resources to bring this about and many fall for the hype and sales-patter of a *'follow the herd world.'* To be free you must become independent and create your own financial resources. You have to be creative and tap into the *market pulse*, although your money making activities must meet your needs and personal values.

This is why working just to keep your creditors happy and pay debts will never fulfil you at the deepest level, nor trigger your genius spark! I am a great believer in the *fluidity* of life and the *flexibility* of circumstances. What you do must make you happy and joyful, beyond feeding your ego and avail oneself away from the gigantic pull of the average wage-slave.

You make the conscious decision about what you accept and where you want your life to be spent. Temporarily accept where you are for now, but work towards freedom. Trying to resist what is (*at this moment*) causes you stress and crushes your energy. When you honour your higher purpose you'll never concern yourself about doing longer hours. Did Jesus ever complain about overtime or working weekends? But beyond healing the sick and fuelling your passion, what you do purely for money, must be as relatively short as possible.

In other words you need to earn as much money as possible for the least amount of time invested to make it happen. If you work for an employer (*or some crazy person, such as yourself*), relying on a salary or set income, then you must look at other ways to escape this trap whist still meeting your needs. Working long unsocial hours, weekends and still thinking about work related issues everywhere you go is a sickness of the mind.

YOUR WAKE-UP CALL!

Often, the only cure for this is usually a high-impact life interruption, such as a tragedy or illness. Otherwise known as the '*wake-up-call!*' This is the last thing you want. As you are reading this book, I can assume you are at the point where change must happen and happen quickly.

The amount of money you need is always relative to your needs and obligations. As your outgoings and circumstances improve you'll need much less. That is as long as your ego is tamed with spiritual *awakening and training*. If your working life is only about paying debts and meeting creditor obligations, this will prevent you from being free, at least in the short term. You will never be totally free financially until you don't owe anything (or vey little) and have little outgoings, where the money you do earn more than covers your needs.

If meeting your obligations causes you a lot of stress, then life can feel like a prison sentence with a release date way off in the future. This of course is a state of mind, which does not serve you. Frustration and stress can lead to illness and a lowered immune system and ultimately health is your highest value, because your body is your transportation vehicle, through which life is experienced and you need it to make money.

PLAN YOUR ESCAPE

What you have to do is plan your escape route in the fastest and least distressing way possible. If you don't make the necessary changes you will end up being dragged along the current of life with the rest of the collective unconscious. Many people are their own worst enemy because they are incessant negative thinkers. They actually start wondering if they are really *good enough* to be free? Or think they are "bound to make a mistake" or keep asking, "am I good enough" or other self-deprecating crap?

Some people think like a fly, trapped behind a windowpane trying to get out. The glass is their thoughts and they are the fly frantically expecting the glass to disappear? In psychology this is referred to as *'learned helplessness.'* Nothing is going to change until *YOU* remove yourself from the glass. The masses treat money and glamour like a god; this has a huge collective pull on the emotions of the people. In a way it's a form of addiction, because many virtually kill themselves in an attempt to keep feeding the monster. Buying stuff, trying to look good, keeping up, consuming more and more, all to keep the entire material illusion going.

Many live their lives in a constant state of 'survival-consciousness,' obsessed with earning money. Afraid they will lose what they have or someone will take it all away. Truth is, everything you have is *temporary* anyway and part of a deep seated fantasy, which says your stuff makes you who you are. Unfortunately, many believe what they see around them is real and attach too much emphasis to pieces of paper and are prepared to go crazy, kill, lie or cheat to get more of it. Some just sacrifice themselves to paper gods.

For a moment, let's just suppose you decide to have tomorrow off and did what you wanted. Nothing stressful on your mind. Nothing bothering you. You spend your day doing what you want to do, instead of being a slave to a job or moronic boss! Maybe you'll spend your day quietly at home, playing sport, relaxing with a good book, go to the park with your kids, meet a friend for a coffee, invite a friend for lunch, or just do nothing. At the end of the day, something extraordinary occurred. Instead of being exhausted, tired and sapped, you feel invigorated. You feel happier and calmer than in a long time.

A NEW REALITY

You've actually begun to feel more alive. It's a day you will never forget! But something else extraordinary happened. You actually made money. While you were enjoying yourself, money came into your life, without too much effort. Next day, same thing happens. You have the day off and money keeps appearing in your account. Day after day, after day! Is this something you'd like more, in your life? Here's the secret to living financially and burden free. The best way to earn money is as *passively as possible*, rather than living your life shackled to an alarm clock (why do you think it's called an alarm clock?). Commuting to work, spending countless hours a day in a job you hate and then coming home depressed? Feeling unappreciated, undervalued, just another number on a spreadsheet! Would you rather take time off whenever you wanted or work a lot less, but still earn enough to meet your needs?

I thought you'd say yes!

Let's move onto the next section and see if we can make it possible...

Power Tip:

1. Don't kill yourself chasing paper
2. Find fluidity and flexibility in all circumstances
3. Don't treat money as a god

Fox Freedom Factor Maxim:

Plan your escape in the quickest and least stressful way possible

Chapter 6:

Work For *<u>More</u>* Money

What you need to do is earn as much money as possible from the activities you do. In other words if you work for 3 hours, you need to ensure you make the most of that time. Wage-slaves seldom make enough and remain trapped in a system that just eats their life. Better still, if you can earn money from something you only do once, such as a royalty payment or recurring income all the better. I am a firm believer in the power of "*Passive Recurring Income,*" which translates to creating systems designed to generate recurring income from something you do just *once*. Obviously, there is the maintenance/looking after side of things you still have to do. What I mean is not going out and getting paid a wage or salary, because as tough as it might sound, completely sucks and does not set you free. In fact in many ways, it keeps you trapped.

To become a physically and spiritually free individual you need to be in the driving seat of your life. Remaining on the mouse-wheel with the majority is neither gallant nor intelligent. Now is the time to change your conditions and feelings about your situation and circumstances, not someday in the future when you perceive things are better. The future starts today in the thoughts you inject into your everyday living and waking moments.

Think about this, if you are trading your time for money, you'll never be free. And even if you are successfully selling a product or service, and you haven't learned how to immediately transform parts of your business into a passive recurring income generator, then you are sub-optimizing your time and income. This is the only way you can *liberate* yourself from stagnation and create your own fulfilling destiny.

NEW THINKERS AND LEADERS ARE RISING

Some may say "yes, but what about the recession?" At time of writing, the world economy has nose-dived over the past few years, because the debt and credit bubble has burst. Virtually the entire global economy is based on debt and money it does not have. You don't have to be an economist to see what's going on. The institutions keep the people trapped and controlled using credit, hoping people will never pay it off, all whilst living off the interest you pay. Don't buy into the illusion of the recession. Yes, the economy is sick, but this is what is needed to cleanse the soul of the planet. New leaders, pioneers and thinkers need to emerge. People will never be free when they are in debt and sometimes you have to lose everything and start again with a new found freedom. Flowers die off in winter, but rise up again in spring to remind us of their infinite simple beauty.

This is another reason why you need to look for recurring multiple income streams in your life. One's that are mostly immune to economic fluctuations. If you are really serious about escaping the rat race, then you need to get out of living in 'survival-anxiety' and being a prisoner of time! When you look at this through the eyes of destiny rather than the shackles of limitation, you'll know it's something you must do.

If you don't take action you will end up experiencing the destiny of the masses. This is millions of people shackled to the system, like robots, enslaved to debt and obligation. So, here's your wake up call. You don't need a JOB; you need to know how to create *Passive Residual Income Streams* in your life, starting now. You don't need another 5 years to teach you the price of procrastination, do you?! Let me tell you a secret of the free:

ONE EFFORT MULTIPLE REWARDS

They all work on the principle of "compound interest." Instead of earning 'X' amount per hour, they earn 'XXX plus' per hour. For the same effort, the same amount of time. One effort = multiple rewards and you should be doing the same! It's the only way to break the cycle and create incredible serenity in your life.

One of the biggest hurdles people seem to have about this, is feeling they don't know enough or have the right resources to escape from where they are? But you'd be amazed at what you can do and create once you step away from the unconsciousness of limited thinking. Your thoughts either attract or repel money and wealth. Money likes stability and security, that's another reason why the rich get richer. If you harbour negative feelings about your lack, all you do is invoke a wave like energy which pushes opportunities away and closes the door to freedom.

Abundance and wealth are *god given* and it's your right to be free from the tyranny of struggle. But no plan, business venture or brainwave will help you until you change your consciousness around money and wealth. Everything else is just plain unnecessary.

Equally you must never take money that seriously, otherwise you'll struggle and what you do have will cause you constant stress and worry. Abundance consciousness hates seriousness, it loves fun and playfulness. It's just a game humans play and you just have to learn to align yourself to being in the right space and place. **Remember this;** *you have in your life what you observe*! What that means, is you only experience what you notice, what you see is what you get. We'll talk more about that later!

You need to work on yourself when you are financially challenged, but like any other situation, needs to be mastered with discipline and being on a higher spiritual path. Never see money as the key symbol of survival in your life, simply view it as a means to an end, a way of buying experience. Not having enough money does not make you a failure. You can only fail when you allow not having much to dominate every aspect of life and consciousness. This is why you should not base your identity solely on what objects you own, as I already said. Yes, money is important in terms of helping you pay your bills and keeping a roof over your head, but most people lock themselves in door-less cages and end up building a more glorified mouse-wheel.

You can decorate your prison cell as much as you like, but it's still a prison cell!

This is why you need to condition yourself to align with abundance and developing recurring income streams, not in terms of taking on more work and doing more, because it isn't going to help you one bit. Unless your goal is to become a victim of Keroshi (Japanese word for dying from over work)?

But having a proper system in place, one that is *recurring* and *replicable*, everything else is just another entry on a long list of activities that don't move you any further forward. If you are prepared to accept and step out of the conditioning of the masses, you will gradually *elevate your personal energy* and circumstances and your life will become simpler and easier.

One of my first lessons in *'recurring do-it-once income'* was a training video I created with a joint-venture partner about leg stretching. I was well known for having an eye-watering level of flexibility in my younger days, so much so I'd been on TV and in newspapers and all that jazz! Back then VHS video was all the rage and we filmed at a friend's house (converted garage type of thing, you know the drill). It took about four hours to film, then fast-forward, once or twice a year I would receive a cheque from the producer in royalty payments. Often the payments were much higher than what I was earning when employed. To use an old cliché, *I began to wake up and smell the coffee!* It began to dawn on me if I could create several of these *"ventures,"* I would not have to work again or at least have more choice in my life.

The amazing thing is YOU can do the same.

Power Tip:

1. Fully optimize your time and resources to create income streams that continue working when you are not!
2. If you are really serious about escaping the rat race, then you need to get out of living in 'Survival Anxiety' and being a prisoner of time!
3. Forget having a JOB; create *Passive Residual Income* Streams that will free you from slavery

Fox Freedom Factor Maxim:

When you raise your creativity you go beyond making ends meet into the realm of natural flow

Chapter 7

You Only Wan
You Observe

When you look around you'll see that everybody is trying to shove their "offer" or product down your throat or make you believe you *can't* survive without it? TV commercials are a classic example of an industry trying to brainwash you into believing you are not good enough and the only way to change is buying their pointless face cream or big-brand product! Have you also noticed how the volume increases during the commercial breaks on TV? This is because they want to get your attention and auditory can be very influencing and attention grabbing to the mind and brain. I like recording things, then fast forwarding the adverts with a wry smile on my face! The advertisers understand the cravings of the human ego and manipulate them to their advantage. They also want to plant seeds into your mind, which are triggered next time you're in the supermarket, where you end up reaching for "that" particular product, which has been cunningly "branded" into your unconscious.

You probably subscribe to email lists of various sorts and receive endless email communications about offers, pitches and promotions. Some of these guys are money-grabbing, power-hungry crazy and although a few might have something useful to say, frankly most are junk. Plus, it's not what you receive that counts, but what you actually USE in your life.

quite often I spend a few minutes dumping a load of lists I thought were once "important!" What you must realise is most *people who have something to say have something to sell!* Not always, however. I am an advocate of personal education and knowledge, because often, what you don't know can hurt you. There are some great people around who can help you to advance to the next level of your life. However, on the whole, people are bombarded with information overload, sending their brain into meltdown!

In theory, the more you learn the better equipped you are in handling life, but the stark reality is 95% of people feel like their brains are exploding with infusion-confusion, brain-dump overload, which is a sure-fire recipe for failure! The only way to handle information is sparingly, if at all? Much of what you read, see, hear and experience, you don't actually use and probably never will. It's always about relevancy. The problem in our society is there is way too much to think about or know about, to which 90-98% is a complete waste of time and irrelevant to your life beyond *"entertainment"* and feeding the ego. You don't need it my friend!

INFORMATION DIETING

Next time you see an advert change the channel, turn down the volume or better still fast-forward. Control the amount of information you receive through the mail or on email. Unsubscribe, delete, and opt-out, whatever it takes. Don't fall for the hype, the glitz, patter and glamour. I often tell sales people what I really think about their pitch or product and their brains blow a fuse because it's not in their script!

When you hear them go erm, arh or they make those "sales-closing" noises at you, you know the ones I'm talking about; that's their *bullshit gland swelling*. Run as quick as you can!

If you see an attractive looking new car and your desire puffs up. Think about the cost, the payments and interest, once the shine has worn off? Today's new thing is tomorrow's out-of-fashion junk. It's easy to get drawn into the ego side of things, but the ego hates self awareness and higher consciousness. This is your best defence against being sucked into an ego controlled existence. At a core level unconscious humans are very much susceptible to the stimulus of the ancient brain, which is the primitive mind. *'Me see, me want!'* Advertisers and marketers know this, which is why they are learning more about how to use the relatively new science of Neuro-Marketing or Marketing Neuroscience. Part of which is selling to your emotions, in other words your *aspirational* ego.

They understand people buy for emotional reasons, not practical ones and then rationalise those decisions with logical reason or whatever they happen to tell themselves to justify their decision. They use two major motivators against you, which are: *PAIN Avoidance and PLEASURE Seeking*. They cleverly manipulate your buying decisions to ensure you associate incredible PLEASURE to buying and relate massive PAIN to not buying their product or service. They do this in some very imaginative and powerful ways. Who wants to be unattractive and considered a loser? They seduce you with music, lights, and decorate the set with attractive looking people or so-called "aspirational" imagery.

Almost making you feel like a complete idiot if you don't act and conform to what they want of you. Marketers spend fortunes finding what *pain triggers* their target market has inside their heads, relating to their product. Then they hammer you with emotional levers and look for your vulnerable spot(s) and then attack them.

I started in business as a Martial Arts instructor because this is my background, beyond this; my passion was and still is for mastering the mind. I have trained fighters to control their thoughts and minds during combat, helping them overcome fear. I created an audio CD combatants can use to place them in the *'power-zone'* prior to battle. I also ran a corporate training company, offering high-hope executives the opportunity to walk on beds of hot coals and break arrows in their throats or smash wooden boards Karate style. Not because their business was failing and they wanted to sacrifice themselves on the ceremonial fires of personal failure, but because they wanted to create a *Zen like* presence in their business and put the fear of god in their enemies. It worked a treat!

THE EYES HAVE IT

Most humans are predominantly visual in their perceptions, it's the way we are wired, and visual stimulus can be very influential. Although decisions are made using the combination of several stimuli, the strongest influence modality is *visual*. This is because humanities first sense was sight. As far as anyone knows, the human brain is about 450 million years old, yet words have only been around for about 40,000 years and yet written language, around for only about 10,000 years.

Here's the interesting thing, the decision making portion of our mind is located in the oldest part of our brain, otherwise known as our *survival brain*. It's easy to see why visual input is our primary decision making filter, because we are hardwired that way.

Some of the ways you can avoid being visually influenced is to close or divert your eyes during a presentation or TV commercial, switch the channel or record your favourite TV shows, like I said earlier. Shop online instead of in-store. You become a master of *selective sight!* When you go into a supermarket you don't have to be a psychologist to see we're bombarded with a plethora of visual stimulus and sensory overload. A friend, who teaches covert persuasion, once told me *some* supermarkets hire attractive people to wander around the store picking up various items and place them in their trolley, only to put them back later. Whether this is true of all supermarkets I don't know, but you can be pretty certain they will do whatever they can to get you to part with your money.

You may say, but that's unethical. Yes, of course, but you could say the same of using music, special lighting, product placement, special offers, celebrity endorsement, buy-one-get-one-free, and a range of other techniques, because they are all designed to influence and manipulate you at some level, aren't they? To them we are all *fair game,* and if they can get away with it they probably will use it!

Power Tip:

1. Trim your life of unwanted and unusable information
2. *Most* people who have something to say have something to sell
3. Don't allow people to manipulate you with the pain lever

Fox Freedom Factor Maxim:

Raise your awareness of how society is designed to control and trap you with clever and subtle Ninja tactics!

Chapter 8:

Stand Guard At The Door Of Your Mind

I have studied psychology and the mind heavily for over 30 years. For this reason; why would you have a built-in *genius-able* bio computer and not know how to use it efficiently? Also, the more you understand about the mind, the more you realise what is being used against you by unscrupulous people and organisations intent on taking your money or locking you into debt burden.

What is amazing is the fact we can be susceptible to ideas or thoughts being planted in our minds, even when we are unaware. This is referred to as 'Perception Without Awareness' or Priming. Priming is exposing a person to certain stimuli, which gets planted in the memory, which then gets triggered at a later date. Think of a tune you hear on the radio or TV and later on you are singing or humming it. TV advertisers use repetition as a form of priming. That annoying jingle, you can't shake come to mind?!

In 1999 Jennifer Mckendrick, Adrian North and David Hargreaves from the University of Leicester held an influence experiment in a local wine shop. They discovered, when French music was played in the shop, 77% of the wine sold that day was French. When German music was played, 73% of the wine sold on the day was German. The nationality of the music was alternated over a 14 day period.

86% of the customers claimed the music made no difference to the wine they chose! *Really!!!* Little did they realise the unconscious affect the music had upon them. Dr North in another experiment demonstrated how music could be used to drastically prime the sense of taste. In this situation, a wine tasting session was created using a background of different types of music. Wine tasting with powerful and heavy music played in the background was described as heavy. Wine tasting with soft mellow music playing was described as, you guessed it, *mellow*. The subject's perception of taste had been *unconsciously shifted* by the background music accompanying the experiment.

EVERYWHERE YOU LOOK SOME FORM OF MANIPULATION IS TAKING PLACE

You are being duped by organisations, marketers and governments intent on shrinking your bank balance and trapping you. Some people claim they don't fall for that sort of thing because they're too *"clued-up."* Interestingly enough, so thought the wine tasters! There are many techniques used these days to influence us, and the more you understand this area the less likely you'll get stung. It's difficult to fight against government policy, depending on how much it affects you, but you can make better choices on how you evaluate information and consumer stimulation.

I love the Chinese proverb:

"You cannot prevent the birds of sorrow from flying over your head, but you can prevent them from building nests in your hair."

This means, although you are going to be exposed to incessant advertising and marketing stimulation, *you are not going to conform like other robots.* It's going to take effort to push against the tide of control and the status quo, but with awareness you can do it. You must control what information you allow inside your mind and stand guard against the garbage people want to place there.

To help give you a better understanding of how you are influenced, here are the top 7 Persuasion Techniques that have been, or are being used against you.

1. Reciprocation:

Often companies will give you something for free as a *teaser* or what they call a *bait piece.* The act of giving something of perceived value often compels you to feel obliged to give something of equal or greater perceived value in return. Many companies give things away, then come to collect later on, when their *generosity* has had time to simmer. A classic example is the use of a free sample or 'taster' in a supermarket. Not many customers feel comfortable about taking the free sample and just walking away, so they reciprocate and buy the product even if they wouldn't normally.

2. Anchoring:

Once a person is in an intense emotional state and something *unique* happens consistently around them, the experience will be anchored to that situation. Savvy salesmen and on-the-pulse marketers will try to get you into the most *resourceful receptive state* possible, then anchor their product or service to that state.

If you can control who and what puts you in a *'buying-state'* you will control who and what influences you, and who and what doesn't. Many advertisers use celebrities in their commercials, because they want to associate the feelings (states) you have to the celebrity and shift those onto the product. They want to transfer the associations people have with those celebrities (wealth, status, beauty, perfection, etc) to their product or service. I call it glamour transference. It's a very crafty and well used technique.

WHO'S RINGING YOUR BELL?

The well known experiment by Russian mathematician Ivan Pavlov, eminently referred to as "Pavlov's Dog," rung a bell every time he fed his dog, which would salivate. Eventually his dog would salivate just at hearing the bell. This is another example of anchoring.

3.　　Rapport:

Companies and marketers want you to like them and their company. They want you to think they really care and are your best friend. They really want to listen to you, long enough to get you to spend your money that is. One guy I had an email from would close the email, saying he really cared about me (I was an address on his list)! I'm all for sharing more love and compassion in the world, but this came across as *artful-manipulation*. Again, advertisers might use someone you already trust and transfer that confidence to their product or service. Just remember the *"artiste"* is being paid, or should I say bribed!

A lot of salesmen have been on NLP (Neuro Linguistic Programming) courses and learn how to 'match and mirror' you. They breathe at the same rate, cross their legs at the same time, pick their nose, etc, use similar gestures to you. If you spot someone trying to befriend (*be-fiend*) you, do something outrageous such as pretend to hear a noise, interrupt them midflow and say "can you hear that?" Keep this charade going for a while. At least, long enough to distort and confuse their sales-script, or rapport building pattern. Breaking someone's pattern is a great antidote to a sales pitch. *Ding! Ding!*

4.   Social Proof:

When someone is unsure of what to do or how to act, they will look to others in the same or similar situation or scenario to see what they do, or how they act. Parallels can be drawn from wanting to conform and is often described as 'the HERD mentality.' Like a herd of sheep, when one move, they generally all move, behaving in the same way – like a good herd of '*sheeple*!'

Advertisers will declare, they have sold thousands of copies of "said" product and "everyone" is jumping on board. This is why brands want to build a community feel to their product and use forums and social networking techniques. Engaging the power of social proof.

You'll see success stories and case studies in their marketing materials, which gently *massages* the mentality of wanting to 'keep up with others!' Well known brands in recent years, have huge PR budgets and sponsor TV programmes and major events. It's all about sponsorship these days! When you open your eyes, you'll be aware of this everywhere you look. "If others like us, so will you?"

5.   Liking:

Marketers use clever techniques to try to make you feel as though they are on your side and really interested in you. They look to create the *"likeability factor."* This also explains why you often see "attractive" people in sales roles or on TV shopping channels or serving behind the bar. Most guys are suckers for the "fluttering eyelashes" technique used by some women to illicit agreement. When a woman smiles at a guy, no matter how innocent, at some level, he thinks she's up for it, in most cases! Of course other things are affected by this, such as how attractive he finds her, and the state of mind he's in at the time. Other elements are also influential with liking such as, similarities, same social group, compliments, noticeable talent, kindness, helping, support, etc.

6.   Scarcity:

Scarcity is probably one of the most *used* persuasion tools, because people are programmed to avoid the feeling of missing out on something. This is why some products and services are deliberately limited. A similar principle to reverse psychology. When unconscious people are told they can't have something, most want it more and are more influenced to try and get it. Similarly, scarcity can be related to the basic principle of supply and demand. Demand for a product or service will increase when there is a limited supply or limited time to get it, etc. *Sheeple* will also pay more to get what they feel is running out. Marketers will manipulate consumers by stirring up competiveness between people by limiting supply. This increases demand and therefore competition, because people want to get it before the *'other guy'* does, and will usually pay over the odds for the privilege.

Limiting stock or using short deadlines always triggers fear of loss or missing out. X-Box, Playstation, Harry Potter and many others have all used the *'limited supply'* technique. This is fed into the marketing process and shows crowds cueing up, and scenes of fervent buyer frenzy, which dovetails with social proof to create a cocktail of powerful compliance inducers on the unsuspecting public.

7.   Emotions:

I've already touched on how emotions play a big part in persuasion and how marketers and advertisers try to *lever* you mentally to get you to buy. For instance a person buys a Range Rover because they WANT it. Not just because it gets them from A to B, but because they WANT everything else it gives them, such as prestige, comfort, and a monumental boost to their already inflated ego.

Next time you are thinking of making a purchase, analyse the reasons why? I remember years ago, going into a Porsche showroom, where the salesman clung to me like spandex. He inaccurately profiled me, by saying the 911 was a "horny car!" To which I replied yes, with a stiff price tag! I quickly left, before we got engaged. To avoid someone levering your feelings and wrestling your mind into their agenda, truly connect with your emotions and be truthful with yourself. It hurts to admit you're trying to boost your ego and looking for people to accept and notice you, but it's a hugely powerful lesson in spiritual growth. The ego hates emotional awareness because they cannot co-exist.

Growing wise is not showing off!

It takes a combination and compounding effort of things to influence someone and other elements can come into play too, which I have not covered here. Just make sure you are aware of what is going on around you. Keep your *BS antenna* open and tuned into tracking the hypocrisy of society. Become more present before making any big decisions and notice any influence techniques being used against you, no matter how subtle or crafty. Forget about past and future when they are of no use. You don't have to prove anything. Open your eyes, cover your ears and close the door to the manipulations of a materially obsessed society.

Power Tip:

1. Open your mind to the subtle use of *"persuasion"* techniques being used around you
2. Notice everything!
3. Don't be a *"sheeple"* be a lion

Fox Freedom Factor Maxim:

Loosen the mental contraction when your expectations are not realised - Make freedom your only goal

Chapter 9

Be Still, Be Silent

One of the greatest gifts you can give to yourself to calm the ego, is *stillness and silence*, being at one with what you have and where you are right now. Maintaining an ever present-presence beyond competiveness and consumerism. You seek what Zen masters call a sacred emptiness. You go beyond ego and the transient gratifications of negative craving. The secret to this is very simple; all you need do is remain *very present* when thinking about feeding your ego or about seeking approval from others. People spend most of their time thinking about the past and the future, projecting their mind into the illusion of some distant utopia; thinking when this or that happens, I will be happy?

Looking for circumstances and situations to make them feel OK. If I buy this new gadget, or if I buy this new car, or this new TV, I'll be happy. This is a complete empty vessel and only serves to enhance the feeling of personal dissatisfaction.
The only power you really have is *choice* and *control* over your perception of things, because perception *IS* your reality. Giving your personal power away is futile. Mastering your ego is the only "thing" that will give you joy and freedom, beyond looking for your sense of self in objects and form. Most of our modern environment is designed to take you away from stillness and silence, into the hubris of consumerism, materialism and activity. Like I said, I have no issue with owning beautiful things and quality items. It's when those things own you, and you're suckered into debt and obligation.

BECOMING MORE SPIRITUAL IS THE ONLY WAY OUT OF PAIN

If you won the lottery, and went out and blew it on a fleet of cars, mansions, gold plated gadgets and designer brands, then *knock yourself out*! But the reality is this, when the shine has worn off, you'll still feel empty inside. Money cannot mask a lack of self-worth or spiritual growth. Besides, money won't give you total security; it will simply change the types of problems you experience. This is why being more spiritual is the only way out of pain and into personal freedom.

Some people think money and spirituality cannot live together, but without money *you cannot be free to relax* into your spiritual quest. *Money makes your spiritual journey more sustainable.* This book is about having what you need to give yourself a sense of freedom and spiritual awareness. Wealth is an attitude, a state of mind and opening yourself up to abundance. You raise your energy and personal vibrational frequency. In other words, you become like the lighthouse, whose beacon becomes brighter and illuminating, attracting the right experiences to you. Experiences, that before, were invisible to a lower realised human.

The other side of the coin is, unless you raise your energy and inner power, you'll run around with the rest of the herd, following everybody else, waiting to be told what to do and where to go by the shepherds of life. *The only real power you have is the potential you have inside.* As you raise your conscious thoughts, silence your mind and ego, you will *pull* the right things towards you, metaphysically speaking.

You'll be in the right place at the right time, and the right people and circumstances will align to the energy you put out.

You won't have to push and shove like others do, day-in-day-out. The sporadic desperations of the market place will not be part of your consciousness. I know from personal experience, the more you push yourself on people and situations, the more you push them away.

This is why I recommend you meditate and practice centering the mind and balancing the body with discipline and meditation. When you react to things or circumstances you weaken your energy and personal resourcefulness. Humans are wired to be reactive when they are not trained and disciplined. This is why advertisers and salesmen love unconscious people, because they are easier to *manipulate into agreement*. They realise most people want what others have, and are trying to be somebody in the world, because they have been conditioned from a very early age to indentify with status, form, money and possessions.

CHASING THE ILLUSION

People endlessly chase after the *illusion* of security in things, such as position, money and status, but that is a fool's delusion. The only way to be really free is to be liberated from ego and debt. Everything else is a trap in one "form" or another. This book is not about meditation or visualisation as such, but I do include some of the exercises I've used and taught over the years. There are some resources at www.ian-fox.com which might also help you.

It's not about being overly "spiritual" or god like. Nor do you need loads of practice to be able to get it.

All you need do is silence and slow the mind and thoughts by directing your attentions and awareness on something simple.

Although there are plenty of marketers and advertisers trying to control you and take your money, there are also many so-called *"spiritual gurus"* who take on an unspiritual erroneous pursuit of paper gods! I'm not knocking anyone for making a living helping others, but I'm sure you know the type? Cheesy gurus with hidden agendas! They use their spirituality as another form of ego massaging. So, if you unfortunately come across any of these, use the same techniques we've already talked about. There are all sorts of ways to practice being still and silent, but please remember being silent is different from being quiet. In silence you are making a conscious decision to refrain from making noise or being subjected to noise.

Being silent could be choosing not to enter into conversation or engage in an argument or ego-motivated, judgemental discussion. It could be, just being silent when you would normally talk, respond or react. Often friends and family will try to draw you into an argument or discussion about something pointless or insignificant. This is where you have to be most aware and conscious. Remembering you *DO* have a choice, in how you respond.

No one can take your conscious choice away.

By being silent and quietening the mind, you are no longer identified with *"things and stuff"* affecting the minds of the masses, because you begin to raise your consciousness out of the hypnosis of egoic satisfaction and stimulation.

You free yourself from the captivity of materialistic recognition and incarceration of endless opinions. You become more aware of the space between your thoughts, rather than the thoughts themselves. It takes practice, but you go one moment at a time.

You don't have to wear robes or tie your hair back, just be yourself. There is no need to be all *"spiritual"* about it by replacing one ego-centric form for another. I have seen so many people who have used their spirituality as a lever to fulfil their holier-than-thou ego's! You are looking to create a deeper sense of inner peace and serenity. This feeling then reveals itself when you are being bombarded with advertising and sales messages, acting as your psychic defence shield. You become very aware of this peace and less disturbed by the wanting ego. The more you can exist in this *space,* the less likely you are to be seduced by the glitz and glamour trapping everybody else.

YOU HAVE TO RESIST THE LURE OF ENDLESS CRAVING

When you are still, silent and in a meditative state, you disengage the ego and control the *"desire"* part of the brain. Technically, you tell the ego to *"shut the heck up!"* It is difficult for a conditioned mind, rampant with thought and craving to slow down and be quiet, but it is possible with regular practice. The truth is, we are all the result of our mental and physical conditioning, but we can change it through different conditioning. *You just have to push through the incredible momentum of "Thought-itis!"*

You'll break free from the ensnarement of thought. After a while you'll gain flow and inner peace, which is not dependant on stimulus from the ego to satisfy it.

65

You also realise you are more than your body, belongings, career, family and bank balance, etc. There is a euphoric *"click"* and the lock is released. Your experience of life will be filtered through the portal of inner calm, and whilst you are free to indulge in the pleasures of modern living, you do not derive your identity from them. Their power is neutralised. Unlike the majority of people, you are not addicted to proving yourself or keeping up with the *"Joneses!"*

Without this inner peace and *deep-knowing*, your life will be overly serious and too much attention will be given to chasing fleeting satisfactions, which to the untrained mind are invisible as they are caught up in the egoic trance illusion. Many people literally kill themselves chasing success. The *sanitised* version of glamour and wealth you see on TV is not the moment to moment reality most experience. Competitiveness, looking for status, being more attractive, etc, is a complete dog-eat-dog trap!

The more you think about having, the more you define what you don't, which is the definition of destruction.

For many people, their lives are clogged up with activity and things to do, stuff to think about, etc, as they live under the weight of every day pressure and tension. But how much of this is actually self-inflicted? How much could be *neutralised* or *released*? This is why people go out and buy things they really don't need, or stuff purchased in the wrong state. I once went to a specialist Japanese drummer concert, and bought their album on CD. I never did play it, not once!

Okay, let's look at a few simple Meditation exercises to help you become more still and silent, which you can do at home:

1: Stare At Candle

A pleasant and easy meditation method is the candle meditation. It's also known as "tratak" or fixed gazing. You can either use it to help you control the ego, or as a meditation in itself. You just place a candle, in a safe holder, on a low table. A coffee table would be perfect. Light the candle, then sit around the candle and gaze at the flame for a few minutes, without thinking of anything. Empty your mind and just spiritually connect with the flame. If any egoic thoughts come into your mind, just say *"I'll come back to you later."* Make sure you blow the candle out when finished and never fall asleep with the candle flame lit, (Ok, health and safety lecture over). Let's move on…

2: Word Repetition

Sit or lie in a comfortable position. Close your eyes and breathe deeply. Let your breathing become slow and relaxed. Focus all your attention on your breathing. Notice the movement of your chest and abdomen, going in and out. Make a conscious decision to push all other thoughts, feelings, and sensations aside for the duration of this Meditation. If you feel your attention wandering, bring your focus back to your breathing. As you inhale, say the word *"calm"* to yourself, and as you exhale, say the word *"relax."* Draw out the pronunciation of the word, so that it lasts for the entire breath. The word "calm" sounds like *c-a-a-a-l-l-l-l-m-m-m*. The word *"relax"* sounds like *r-e-e-l-l-a-a-x-x-x*. Repeating these words as you breathe will help you to concentrate.

Continue this exercise until you feel very *calm* and *relaxed*. Over time, you will notice you will be able to elongate the words as your breath becomes more developed. Try with other words to focus on such as colours.

3: Awareness Meditation

Take a few deeper, slower breaths if you like, but then let your breathing come back to its natural rhythm. Now bring the awareness to feel your sitting posture, how your body is placed. Spend a few minutes just letting the awareness move through the body, starting where the buttocks are touching the floor, just feeling the hardness or softness of that contact. Then, let the awareness move through the legs, feeling the way they are bent, where they touch the floor or chair, and the touch of the clothes on the skin, etc. Slowly let the awareness come all the way up through the body, just feeling all of it, allowing the different sensations to come and go. When you arrive up in the face area, feel where the lips are touching together, feel the wetness or the dryness, the softness; feel the tongue resting in the mouth; feel the air going in and out of the nostrils; feel the eyelids resting on the eyeballs, feel the eyes in the sockets and the muscles around them. Really experience these sensations. Feel the hair on the head, where it may touch the ears or back of the neck or shoulders, or enjoy the baldness of your exposed crown.

Now, from the point on the top of the head, let the awareness drift down through the body. Become aware of the general outline of the entire sitting posture in an attitude of *"over-seeing awareness,"* as if the awareness were resting slightly behind the body. Imagine a healing energy, like the rays of the *Sun;* begin to flow over the body as you absorb its warmth and all-embracing power.

This is a powerful body-meditation, which really connects you with *body presence* in one unique method. Because the body is how we experience the world and all it offers, and the body is the vehicle in which we experience the universe and its infinite powers, connecting with body-awareness is hugely potent in our spiritual development. Yet, most meditations and spiritual knowledge attempts to remove oneself from the body.

The Story of Zen Attention!

"Master, I dream of everlasting happiness. What is the highest wisdom you can teach me?" asked the student. The Master smiled. He took his brush and wrote as if for the first time, "Attention." "Wonderful," said the student, "And what comes next after attention?" he asked. The Master smiled. He took his brush and wrote, as if for the first time "Attention, Attention." "Yes," nodded the student, utterly perplexed. "Anything more?" he asked... The Master smiled. He took his brush and wrote, as if for the first time "Attention, Attention, Attention" "Okay, so what does 'attention' mean?" asked the student, unable to see. The Master spoke. "Attention means attention." "Is that all?" said the student, obviously dispirited... "Attention is all," said the Master. "Without attention, happiness is nowhere; with attention, happiness is now here. Attention is freedom from all. Attention offers all."

The bottom line is this, unless you tame and centre the mind with *deliberate stillness* and *controlled silence* you are at the mercy of circumstances and unconscious people. You'll be drifting along like a cork on the ocean. Following the current, being tossed around, and ultimately being washed up on the island of despair! Once you align with the *space* between your thoughts and *inner awareness* of what is going on, you become more conscious of being less materially driven—standing back, viewing events from afar instead of being on the inside looking out.

Power Tip:

1. Unlike the majority of people you are not addicted to proving yourself or keeping up with the *"Joneses!"*
2. Centre your thoughts and *calm* the mind
3. See what was previously invisible

Fox Freedom Factor Maxim:

As they say on London Tubes… "Mind The Gap!"

Chapter 10:

Let Go And Grow

The ego has a hard time letting go of things, people and events. The fact is, nothing you own is yours anyway and you'll leave it all behind one day. You are the manifestation of your thoughts, feelings and experiences. You are part of the collective global *'one consciousness'* and *'infinite mind.'* Money can only ever buy experience, and I don't just mean the *illusionary* momentary feelings of buying an expensive item, or wanting to show off to your mates or peers, etc. The experience I am talking about here is that of raising *one's consciousness* and *self-awareness* beyond feeding your perceptions with BS!

REMEMBER, IT'S ALL AN ILLUSION

The only thing you really want to experience is freedom and liberation, from being chained to the system. Like I said, your mission is not to obtain things because they end up obtaining you, but to operate from a position of *zero restriction.* Experiencing a deep sense of release and the ability to make better personal choices about what you do everyday. That is what you are looking for! See your life as a quest for freedom, not as a constant battle to get new things and meet obligations.

This is why you must let go of objects, possessions and life's crud.

People spend vast amounts of time, energy and money trying to keep up with an overweight identity based upon the assumption the quality of their life is the quality and quantity of their possessions, "what I own." When in fact, what you think you own is not yours at all, but the ego's definition of self. It is only when you realise, nothing or *no-thing* has any meaning above that which you attach to it, do you gain freedom.

When you resist letting go of things and holding on, your life becomes a means to an end, therefore you will never be free or happy. You reinforce the ego's control over you and firmly lock yourself into restriction. You become a reactor of circumstances and bounce from one object to another, fully associating with covetousness. Lost in a sea of confusion and object led delusion. When you let go, you release yourself from bondage to things. Free from the mind's patterns, structure and conditioning. You begin to exude a silent strength.

This all forms part of the *letting go process*. You start with small things and then build up. You don't have to give up the things that do make your life easier, just the extraneous crud. By letting go, you unleash a great power few humans will ever experience in their lifetime, other than perhaps at the moments before they die. This means letting go of resistance to things. When you do this, you raise your spiritual power and escape from the *prison of material-form and thought-form*.

When you are totally attached you're not free, but locked in a pseudo reality, which on the surface appears solid and real. Life becomes a fight for survival in a congested universe. The reality is, when you can let go of things, you are not running with everybody else and you don't have to perform or win approval. Sit back and let go–because you are more *powerful* than you could have ever imagined.

NON REACTION

The true master acts out his or her ability in their every action. So it is a powerful eye-opening realisation, when you experience the negative resistance of letting go. It is not necessarily a bad thing, because there is neither good or bad, it just is! One of the many mantras I teach students is that of DNR (Do Not React). When a *"modern living"* challenging scenario arises, which could place you in a reactive state, simply repeat *'Do Not React'* to yourself over and over, and combine this with deep breathing, until the *unconscious* part of the reaction has passed.

In reality, it's more difficult to control DNR when you are in an emotional state or circumstances and people "test" you. This however, is the best time of all to practice the power of DNR. Try it on smaller situations and circumstances, then on life's bigger things. You'll be amazed at the spiritual portal which opens when you are *non-reactive*. You choose what your response will be.

You may not be able to control the situation, but can take control how you respond to it.

Many adorn their lives with possessions (interesting word "possession!"), and although some might have their uses and make your life more comfortable, most are simply set-decoration and imbue an energy of constraint, control and containment. By releasing yourself from their pull and weight you gain fluidity in your life. This does not mean giving your car away (unless there is debt obligation attached to it?) and walking, although that could work for you? Change is quite often dramatic and for many the only way to create a new life.

You have to stay in balance to meet the needs of your current reality, until such a time the new energy takes over and sets you free. The last thing letting go should do, is create more stress in your life. Having said that, *there is no change without challenge*. Letting go of things gives you a huge affirmation, which says "*I am in control*" not the corporations, institutions, circumstances or situations.

Your life shrinks or expands in direct proportion to your ability to choose the right response at any given time. When you are unconscious, any one person or thing can control you. That's when life can become more painful than blissful, and reason why many resort to false stimuli such as food, smoking, drugs, quick-fix sex, to mask the feeling of discomfort. This then becomes an unconscious pattern that pulls you deeper and deeper into the circumstantial quicksand.

If you are aware enough, you can catch yourself right before the reaction takes place or actually in the process itself. Either way, this *raised awareness* is the gateway to higher consciousness and enlightenment, provided that is, your raised awareness is not a fleeting occurrence. Hone your self-awareness through training on the battlefield of human unconsciousness. Interestingly, your friends, family and work colleagues become your teachers and finger pointers. And what is it they teach?

How to understand what it means to be self aware, and step out of the groove of negative reaction and emotion.

You can't blame people for being unconscious and unaware, and it would be pointless trying to change them, besides the very moment you try to change or improve people, you've just slipped into unconsciousness yourself. It's impossible for anyone to change, unless (but not always), they experience a huge *"wake-up-call,"* or until they are at the point of *alignment*, which is being spiritually ready. You may help them with the process of change, but might not be the catalyst.

The incredible feeling letting go offers, is the *real you* and this space between having and not having is the portal, through which you can discover your essential nature free from ego, judgement, labelling and object identification. The question is, are you conscious enough to recognise this within yourself and then do something about it?

Power Tip:

1. Don't get too serious, because it's *all an illusion!*
2. Make your life a quest for freedom
3. What you resist persists

Fox Freedom Factor Maxim:

Do not react, but choose your response based on your primary purpose to let go

Chapter 11:

Master Your Own Conscious-Reality

The SAS have a saying that goes *"Knowledge Dispels Fear"* and this is true. The problem is most people's fear dispels their knowledge. Whenever you are afraid you cut yourself off from the part of you that holds your wisdom. Mostly fear is ego based and materially projected, that is to say, you are afraid of losing your "things." This could be your job, relationship, your money, your life identity, your belongings, etc. This then pulls towards you, the thoughts and circumstances which resonate with the fear emotion.

Depending on the circumstances, *action kills fear.* The thoughtform surrounding the emotion of fear is usually disproportionate to the reality of the fear itself. Meaning, your fear is not as real and solid as it feels or appears at the time, but a bubble of thoughts, feelings and physiology wrapped around an external event or object.

Fear creates personal suffering, which also translates to suffering for others, as you endure the unconsciousness part of fear and become totally identified with the fear itself. Unmanaged fear is one of human kind's greatest challenges, and forms the foundation on which virtually all global suffering originates.

As you practice the meditation exercises I gave you earlier, you should also imagine you are breathing away your unconsciousness, as well as the layers of your identity, and then your false fears will start to untangle.

YOU CREATE AND SHAPE YOUR REALITY

The quality of your life is how you define yourself and how you react to your circumstances. In essence you create your own reality based on your thoughts, perceptions, associations and references. The truth is this, what you see around you and experience on a daily basis is *not real*, it's the fabrications of someone else's idea of what society and life should look like. It's like you are being dragged along with the current of the masses. A lost soul surrounded by a herd of *sheeple*!.

In an object and reactive based existence everything seems to conspire against you and the "system" has a vested interest in keeping you trapped. Partly because the system has been allowed to control and shape your lifestyle. *Your ultimate destiny whilst being alive is to become free,* because without freedom you remain imprisoned by conformity and limitation. Circumstances are one the biggest prisons for most people, with lack of financial resources one of the most difficult to endure. Once you get out of ego and transcend the worship of materialism, you are one step closer to taking back control.

Your perceptions of reality changes, immediately you realise nothing is *that important* or to be taken *that seriously*. External events happen, but *you have a choice* how you respond to them internally. I once had a student who said "every time I do yoga I cry." I said, "then you should stop pushing so hard. It is not the yoga making you cry, but the crud of your life rising to the surface of your consciousness.

This all forms part of your dysfunction. All the self doubt, the past failures, the lack of self belief, the pain from the past is imbued in every asana you practice." I suggested she commit to loving herself more when she practiced, and really enjoy and embrace the relationship between herself and the yogic spirit. I told her; "you are the epitome of yogic force, the tune on which the yogic dance unfolds. There can be no yoga without the yoga practitioner, no music without the instrument." In that moment she ascended to a higher dimension, whilst remaining rooted like a tree.

What you must remember is you're either living your own reality or part of someone else's.

To a certain degree, people are herd animals and live in pens of confined reality. Encased in the illusion created by their thoughts, perceptions and emotions, etc. Their lives or circumstances represent the many knots on a rope, and for some becomes the rope which eventually hangs them. Mastering your reality, means you align your thinking to go beyond mere survival and the ritualistic crap of everyday living. You decide what something means, you don't just slip into unconscious reaction.

You step away from the routines and thought-forms of the masses. Yes, you maintain paying the rent or mortgage, because right now you have little choice, until such a time you become free. The difference is the journey you are taking now becomes one of *applied self-created truth*, and not accepting someone else's restrictions. Yes, you may have to tow the line for the moment, but not indefinitely, just until your plan is realised.

Despite all the emotional/psychological nuances that exist, there are only two states which really matter, they are; *consciousness and unconsciousness*, or put another way *awareness and unawareness*. You are in one of the two at any given moment. The experiential reality of each of these states can make a hugely significant difference to your life and to those around you. To master consciousness means you accept this moment unconditionally, without reservation or resistance. You actively endeavour to move away from unconsciousness, which is total identification with the conditioned mind.

TRANSCEND THE IMPOSSIBLE

When you do this you discover a godlike power few have ever experienced in this world. Thought and habitual thinking keep you trapped in unconsciousness. This does not mean you allow anything to happen in your life, and people to walk over you.
It means you become more aware of what you think, say and do, especially when problems and challenges occur, as they will. *What you can't overcome you have to transcend.* Once you do this you will feel incredibly alert, like you have awoken after a very long sleep. It also takes away any controlling or manipulative power people can have over you through control, egoic-manoeuvring and prejudice.

When you see a situation, person or event as the cause of your pain you remain *stuck*. It may appear this way, but the real cause is your *resistance to the situation*. The mental contraction, the emotional turmoil, and the holding on to it. These are the things causing you pain. It is also rooted inside the emotion of fear. Fear created by the perceived or actual loss of something? Becoming more conscious is a portal to inner awakening, which in essence is a powerful step towards freedom.

This is another reason why material objects will never make you truly happy, because they do not awaken you. In fact they play their part in keeping you deeply unconscious and trapped. This also explains why many business millionaires and "show-business stars" remain heavily unfulfilled and trapped in *doing* rather than *being*. So, your perception of reality is inextricably connected to your level of awakening. Getting more, having more and working hard to achieve material objects will never be truly fulfilling beyond a temporary quick fix, because this does not create an awakening and raise your consciousness.

Money does not take away pain, it just changes the cause. Only by being more spiritually conscious will you ever find true freedom.

The process of raising *conscious-reality* can take time, but remember there is no rush. Rushing and pushing implies struggle, which is unconscious. You'll know you are becoming more awake, when you are not lost in thinking about things – but becoming more aware of your own presence and subtle feelings. It starts with little things then expands and expands as your consciousness grows. You'll see! Work on certain areas of your life which could be easily fixed, then later when you have more confidence, move on to the bigger stuff. You become like the stonemason, slowly chipping away at the crud of your life and relinquishing yourself from the burden of your past mistakes and life-experience.

The more you awaken, the less locked in the ego you'll be, because you'll realise you are the genesis of your reality no matter what shape it takes. You'll become more aware of your thoughts and motives, and the underlying pervading essence of your life will be filtered through higher awareness.

You become more aware and less reactive. You become the master of reality, than the servant of ego. In a way this is like your "*light-bulb*" moment, but on a spiritual level. You peer into another dimension, which is hidden from most people's reality. You feel alive and full of joy without having (or needing) something external to stimulate you. Once this happens, you will not want to go back. Like toothpaste, I mentioned earlier, impossible to put back. But if at the point you read this, your mind tries to contradict it, this is the ego panicking. It really does hate self-awareness. But *push through the bubble of struggle!*

A student once said "I am afraid of rats," when we were speaking of fears. I said "when you take away your mental labels there is no rat and no fear." He said *"there is no fear because there is no rat."* I said, "there was no rat in the first place!" The rat is a mental construct, a collection of sense perceptions; albeit misinterpreted. It is not the rat you fear, but the fear that you fear. All fears are created in the mind and projected onto objects, situations and people. In many ways the rat has more consciousness than the person fearing it, because it does not need therapy to get over the person who fears it. It lives in the here and now.

CONSCIOUSNESS IS THE SECRET GATEWAY OPENING.

You have awoken to the power you have inside you, the gift you were born with, which western life tried to squeeze out. No more excuses, no more unconsciousness. Now is the time for focus, letting go and bringing more light into your life. You go beyond style, fashion and art. You are now more conscious of the ego within you.

Here's the truth; all you ever need is *conscious-awareness*, because this is the only constant, and the one thing you can totally control.

Meditate on that for a few minutes before reading on...

What you are really doing is becoming conscious of the moment before your thoughts and mind take over. You are creating your reality, because you are conscious of yourself before thoughts, perceptions, and conditioning of the world have come into play to diminish, dilute and pollute your awareness.

Nature teaches us many things and animals can become portals through which to observe consciousness. Recently I saw a Buzzard in the sky. I thought, what is the level of the Buzzard's consciousness? Then I thought, what would it say if I asked; *"what its plans were"* (assuming it could talk)? *"What plans"* would be the reply? Observing nature makes you observe the presence in yourself and you should often seek time away from synthetic settings and unconscious people. I have done meditations and healings in the great Pyramid and Temples of Egypt and nothing is more powerful. Once you become more conscious of your own reality, things are never the same again, because you open up a new dimension.

Come let's look at a financial freedom plan of action...

Power Tip:

1. Fear keeps you trapped until you *face it*
2. Free your mind with conscious awareness
3. Work on little things then grow from there

Fox Freedom Factor Maxim:

Your reality is your awareness of perception and self, before thinking has occurred

Chapter 12:

Your Financial Freedom Plan

The irrevocable truth is usually you'll never really be able to earn enough money by working for someone else, plus you'll have to conform and take orders. Remember you're not looking for a job, no matter how much it pays, because of what we've covered already. No price is worth losing your freedom for. There are easier, quicker and more lucrative ways to make money without all the hassles and egos. But again, it depends on what your total monthly financial outgoings are? If you spend more than you earn, you're going to struggle. This is why you need to bring things as much under control as soon as possible, or use what extra money you earn to pay off your debts. Lowering your outgoings as quickly as possible brings you a step closer to taking back control. It may be necessary to keep your regular job temporarily, or whatever you do to earn money now, and use any extra as part of the longer plan for freedom.

The way you earn money though, must form part of your goal to be free, not create another trap or perpetual time drain. There is no use starting a business which saps your energy and power day and night, making your life no better than if you worked for another lunatic! Forget hiring staff, this is a massive headache and the last thing you want is start managing egos.

I've had staff in the past, but never again! I had several *unconscious* Martial Arts instructors who seemed to think, because they taught the students they belonged to them, so off they went leaving me high and dry. In the end, they soon realised being the captain of the ship is very different and more challenging than being a shipmate. Often the "grass is greener" turns out to be the patch were the dog urinates! The reality is they actually did me a huge favour and inadvertently unlocked another shackle around my leg.

In order to get paid you either have to have a *service* or *product* you can sell or *skill-set* people will buy from you. The problem with selling a skill is that you have to be there and deliver, which means commitment and obligation. This also compromises your earning potential, because you can only be in one place at once and will eventually run out of time. It depends on the skill of course, and how much satisfaction you get beyond just being paid. One of the things that few people indulge in is service to others.

There is nothing nobler than giving of self to help others. The ultimate *spiritual testament* is giving selfless acts of kindness and caring that go without the person being recognised for it. This is the true test of how evolved you are? It's called *'Anonymous Giving!'* Of course your giving can only reach so far. The problem can be when contributing creates negative imbalance in your own circumstances.

If you derive acceptance identity through what you do, then there will come a time when this will end and unless you are prepared, will suffer on some level. The advantage is, if you dominate your chosen niche and give more than the competition, as well as control what you do and who you do it for, then you can secure for yourself an income that serves you.

85

This all depends on the skill-set and what you have to do to make it work?

The main problem is most people are in a crazy rush to "*make it,*" ("making it" is an illusion of course) and not prepared to take the required steps and actions to develop a skill or product they can sell. This is indicative of the fact they are financially burdened and pressured to meet ongoing obligations or try to force change in their lives. This often impels them to make quick, knee-jerk decisions and reactions, which do not serve their highest potential. It is amazing just how creative and productive you can become when not pressured or rushed.

TAKE AWAY THE STRUGGLE

The reason why so many struggle is because they are giving out what the masses are offering and competing with everybody else. Nothing sets them part. The "*wash-and-go*" society in which we live has programmed people to look for quick fixes and express routes to the "top!" As you start to awaken you'll see this everywhere. There is no cheat-sheet which guarantees you a place on the podium. You have to be clear on your plan and take specific actions to bring about the results you are looking to create.

You also need to *get-real* on what really suits your personality and experience. I have seen so many people who started businesses and ventures which did not agree with them, only to struggle and eventually fail.

There must be synergy between who you are and what you choose to do.

One of my favourite money-making strategies is:

Make as much as you can for doing something once or at least whenever you do it, maximise your potential to earn.

Let's say you spend an hour offering something, why make 5.00 per hour, when you can make 50.00? Why make 50.00, when you can generate 100.00 per hour? And why settle for 100.00, when you can make 500.00? Makes more sense doesn't it? This is one of the reasons I taught Martial Arts for years, because not only was it something I did well and had a passion for, but also because it paid well and was scalable. However, the main problem was the fact it meant I had to be there, and everyone depended on me, which was okay for a while. When you are good at something it's much harder to back away and focus on other things later on. In a way you become trapped by your own creation.

This is one of the reasons I trained others to teach, but I've already told you what a pain that was! I gradually evolved out of teaching Martial Arts and tapped into my creative side by developing certain fitness workouts, which could be packaged and sold to instructors under licence. Originally I used to travel around the country delivering 1-2 day training courses in these licensed concepts, but this rapidly became another bind.

My eureka moment came when I decided to film all of the instructor training courses and offer them on home-study DVD, audio and PDF. This meant people could buy them from my website (foxfitness.co.uk), pay online, download the audio and instructor guide, and then get sent the DVD package in the mail. Brainwave or what! *Revolution concept actually!*

If you are looking to package and sell the right skills, you can always buy them in or by taking training. My suggestion would be, if you are selling your skills, you must be able to easily deliver them and maximise your chances to earn good financial rewards for the same efforts invested. The skill you offer must be unique (*or have a different slant*) otherwise you'll be competing again with everyone else. One of the ways you can separate yourself is package it differently, or offer more than others do. Become a conduit of *high value service* and inject more *energy* into your services than anyone else. Stand out from the crowd.

But always keep in mind you are looking to create more freedom in your life, not gold plate the shackles.

If offering a service is not your cup of tea, then you could look at selling information. Why information? This is the information age and more and more people are looking to learn things, and more importantly, willing to pay you for it. You won't be surprised to hear; I took a lot of what I knew about Martial Arts and turned it into an info-product, several in fact. *What* do you know that others might like to learn? *Who* do you know that you could do a joint-venture with and split the profits? I heard about a guy who created a dog training DVD and made over £100K, even though he knew nothing about the subject?

Apparently he knew a local dog trainer and asked them to work with him on a training DVD, doing a 50/50 split after expenses had been deducted. He sold it mainly on pay-per-click. It's not always about what you know, but what *who you know, knows!* Does that make sense? Having the mind-set which says *"how can I make this work,"* is an essential component to making money.

The Information selling business is in my view one of the best businesses to be in today. I have been selling information products since 1985 and attest to the fact that information directed towards a niche market, packaged and delivered in the right way, can be the golden ticket to financial freedom.

Selling information can be outrageously simple because you don't need a PhD in ideas to get started. Many info products take what is already out-there, but take on a new twist or creative angle. You need no staff, no direct selling, no premises, no large stock to carry (zero if it's a digital product), little or no start up cash and the risk is quite minimal! With digital products such as e-books, MP3 audios, online courses and membership sites, etc, you could make money 24 hours a day, everyday, come rain or shine! The profit margins are great.

THE ULTIMATE PROFIT STREAM

Some people promote products, which sell for about $27 and cost less than $2-$5 to create. Plus, they can sell them over and over again, because once set-up, they don't have to be there! This means your energy levels are intact and less drained. The *ultimate* way to profit in the information business is this:

1: Find a target market
2: Convince them to buy
3: Offer them more things to buy from you

As the marketing adage goes:

"It's much easier to sell MORE to an existing customer than it is to keep finding new ones."

Your information business stands a better chance of long-term success if you can offer your customer list a related higher value product. It is better to have a series of products you can sell to the same person, than it is to keep trying to sell one product to a new person each time. Makes sense right? If your head is spinning right now, don't despair, because I have some tools to help you. The main thing for you to do now is align yourself with the possibility you can do this, and there is a way to make it happen.

Don't fret, you can still be spiritual and make money, because what you are offering is useful and helpful to the buyer. You are not just pushing to make a few extra quid or bucks. What you offer is born out of a deep desire to add value and help people. Not coerce them into parting with their money for the sake of it. Besides on an energy level this wouldn't work at all, because circumstances would conspire against you. There are people who make money out of greed and ego, but eventually a dark energy descends upon them in the form of illness, loss or suffering or all the above. Chasing money is a lost cause because you can never have enough to satisfy the ego if it's in control of your life.

In essence you have to choose a niche or target market, create a product to sell, and *exchange-info-for-money,* then you'll have your own information income business. What you have to remember, this is not about you becoming rich or living the *"millionaire lifestyle,"* because this is a fantasy fuelled by the ego. There are a lot of people who have bought into that *BS* illusion! This is about making enough money to become free, not feed your ego and collect more shit!

The best way, is to first earn enough to meet your current outgoings and obligations; this takes the pressure off and gives you more space to plan and create. Then you'll use the extra to pay off debts and build a safety net to fall back on. Your money goals may involve helping others, which is great, but believe me; it's much easier to help other people when you are first coming from a place of personal balance yourself.

The biggest hurdle for you is getting started, and gaining momentum, because most people are put off by what seems a daunting task at first. This is because they think in huge chunks and should take baby steps instead of giant leaps. The other bug-bear is the negative thought which says, "what do I know that people would pay for?" But you do know things which are of value to someone, and when you package them right and understand the process of making it work; it becomes much easier to get your head around.

The first thing you need to think about is a market to sell to. But there are some considerations when choosing an ideal market to start your info-business.

Let's look at those:

1: The first thing is a market comfortable with spending money. It's no use trying to sell to a market that is broke or does not value enough what you offer. For instance most golfers are always paying out for the latest contraption, club, or newest technique to improve their handicap. There are a lot of egocentric golfers out-there! Golf is one example, but there are literally dozens when you take time to think about it.

2. You need a market you can sell multiple things to. If all you have is a one-time buyer, you are forever locked in a perpetual cycle of "seek-and-sell!" The best way is to choose a market whereby you can promote a series of offers which are in some way connected with their initial purchase.

3: It is better (but not always) to choose a market you are interested in or have a passion for. If you understand the market already, things are easier and you can work on project development with some level of insider knowledge. When you *"click"* with something from the beginning your starting position is accelerated and your progression optimised.

Some of the people I have worked with over the years have had impressive results by choosing a broad market such as "weight loss," "business opportunity" and "personal relationships," etc. They have then drilled down to create niche products within these markets. The biggest step for you is getting started and coming up with ideas and setting up the process.

In a nutshell this is what you need to do:

1: Decide on a market and do your research
2: Create a product (e-book, report, audio, etc)
3: Build a delivery system (online is best to save fulfilment costs and reach a greater market)
4: Market the product (online/offline marketing)
5: Take the money (PayPal, etc)
6: Repeat the process
7: Use the money to become free

Caution: Step 7 is usually mistaken for buying more *"stuff"* and pandering to egoic pleasures.

From my own experience:

If I can't easily see the market and how easy/hard it is to penetrate, I tend to choose a different one.

You have to get started somewhere and build up slowly, it's a learning curve, but one which should pay off if you are serious and take the required steps in advance. One of the missing elements in most people's money-making endeavours is creativity. Being creative alone will not ensure success, you must have a product or service people are looking for and more importantly will want to buy.

GET CREATIVE

You can really enhance your chances by adding *creative flair* to your offering. A different way of presenting your product, e-book, audio, or perhaps your business has a *JCB on the roof!* The reason I mention the JCB, is because years ago I used to visit a pub with just that! It had a digger on the roof and was aptly named *"The Excavator."* The funny thing is people would avoid sitting directly under where the JCB was positioned. As far as I know, it never actually fell on anyone. The point is, get creative to differentiate yourself from other people. It's pointless putting out what everybody else does.

Although external things my help stimulate you, creativity comes from within. It's difficult being creative when you are being pulled around like a prize bull at the country show by people and circumstances. To find your creative source you have to be still and allow your creative powers to rise, usually following a good night's sleep or following a deep meditation. Remember this, *to be creative get meditative!*

The other point about being creative is be careful your creativity is not locked too much in ego and has a down side of negative obligation and excessive commitment. Perhaps your creativity is just raising the energy of an otherwise boring and mundane looking product, but doing it in a way which has never been seen before.

The P.S.A. Formula

Over the years, I discovered there are simple things you need to keep in mind and focus on to make anything work. This is especially true for info-products and the more complicated something is, the less likely it will be effective and sustainable.

LET ME INTRODUCE YOU TO THE P.S.A. FORMULA:

P is for Products:

If you are going to be financially free and build a worthwhile sum of money to meet your needs and bring about your new *'shackle-free'* lifestyle, then you need to have more than one product you can sell, as I've already said. It's important to start off slowly when you're new at this and create a *'product-project-action-plan'* you can roll out for each new product you want to market.

You need a regular schedule of products you create and deliver to the market. The main reason for this is some products might not yield as much as others? With more than one, you collectively gain financial buoyancy.

S is for System:

For anything to succeed you must follow a system, one that can be easily *replicated* over and over again with just a little tweaking here and there. When you have created an optimal system, your efforts and time are reduced, because you can technically *'run the system'* each time you launch a new product.

> *The backbone of all successful businesses is successful systems.*

A is for Automation:

If you are really going to be free without simply transferring one shackle to another, then your system must run on autopilot for most of the time. There is no such thing as a 100% automatic system though, because somebody's got to do the mundane stuff. There will be product creation, order fulfilment and processing to consider, etc, but this needs to be kept to an essential minimum. I know of many people who create products, then become obsessed with making money, sitting in trance like states, staring at their PCs all day and night.

What you need to remember is the word PC could also stand for *"Possessive Control."* Automation is click to order, instant download, email notification of payment received, etc. Barebones minimum time and energy required. This is one of the reasons I favour online business over other forms of income generation. The good thing about it is you are not tied to a desk or clock watching all day long, nor do you have to work with some ego filled moron or what I call an *"egoron."*

It's amazing how you can be out for the day, later check your email, and then smile as you have received orders. It truly is quite *overwhelmingly fabulous!*

OFFER SOLUTIONS

When you are earning in this way, your attitude and life takes on a new meaning. You become more enthusiastic and your creativity shines brightly. You are doing something you love to do and getting paid for it! A new joy emanates from you, which will in effect; pull better situations and circumstances towards you. What I call an *'attraction energy.'* Ultimately with info-products, or anything you want to sell for that matter, it always comes down to solving problems. People are looking for solutions to the problems they have and the pain they feel, and will pay for someone like you to solve them.

If a problem exists, then you could provide a solution in the form of a product. Once you provide your solution, you can then look for the next problem to solve that person has? This is the typical 'sales' cycle you could create. Your creativity and receptivity will allow you to locate the "sufferer," diagnose the problem and prescribe the solution. In the form of your product(s) of course! Also, you could look at some of the problems you've had over time and solutions you discovered. Is there any leverage there?

When you become a 'solutions provider' you are considered the *go-to-person* and a *trusted* source of valued information. Caveat: When looking for a problem to solve, you must keep in mind the *"Small Wants Little Needs"* philosophy. It's no use looking for problems that are just too big to solve or create a shed-load of hidden problems for you. Keep it simple, keep it quick, and keep it profitable.

IT'S ALL ABOUT TIMING

Mostly, success is about timing. Being in the right place at the right time or bringing something to market at the right time. It's also about developing your sixth sense about up and coming trends and being one step ahead of the lifecycle of a new fashion. Sometimes, watching and waiting is key. If you try to force a need on people they could reject it and you end up wasting a bucket load of energy and time. This leads to frustration and drains your creative edge. If you can create flow to your projects and construct effortless production, then you're doing well.

When I launched one of my first licensed workouts; 'Kick-aerobics' I was spot on timing wise. Billy Blanks's TAE-Bo® was starting to gain in popularity and the trend was growing. One business card size ad in a national magazine would end up bringing in over 30 bookings per 1-day course I ran. I was first in the market and took the initiative whilst others were still dilly-dallying. They choked on the dust of my results! This was about *knowing* the market, *reading* the trends, *taking* action and *getting* the timing right. The rest was cleaning up! Today (at time of writing) the fitness trends are Kettlebell, Zumba, Pole-Dancing and MMA (Mixed Martial Arts) Fitness to name but a few! As I write this, I have already begun my next project, which you can see at: www.mmatrainer.co.uk!

There is a world of difference between creating a home-study instructor training course and trotting off late Friday night or early Saturday morning to deliver the live programme, coming back late and exhausted, then repeating the same thing the following weekend. The distinction is on par with how the word processor revolutionised the type writer!

This is one of the main reasons I favour information products in digital format than any other, primarily because they accelerate your journey to a freedom lifestyle.

FOCUSING YOUR MIND

What you need to do is take a little time to brainstorm your ideas and things which interest you. You'll quickly discover you know more than you realised about certain things, and the floodgates of information begin to open. This is where you start writing things down. *If it's worth doing it's worth writing down.* Some ideas you have may not have legs as yet, but by recording them you can revisit at a later date when the thought just might come to fruition. This has happened so many times for me in the past.

Some ideas could be:

* You've lost weight, but did it in an unusual way or have specialist knowledge that others could use too?

* You have a secret recipe for healing soup or a concoction which cures the common cold?

* You know some unique ways to integrate cats with unruly dogs?

* You know how to create an extra two hours a day using an extraordinary time management system for parents?

These are just some of my *off-the-cuff ideas,* but *your* creativity pool is frankly bottomless. You just need to create the space and environment in your life where your creativity can shine through. Then start capturing the ideas.

Relax into the creative zone without forcing things to happen, if you try to get creative and nothing happens, there's the sign you need which says; flow is not occurring in that moment.

Don't force it, pause it.

When you have some ideas, which look as though they could be fruitful, the next thing to do is the following:

1)   Research the idea online and its correlating market, to see if it could be a winner

Remember, people need to have existing pain and be looking for a solution. If you have to educate or push your product on people, you're inviting struggle into your life. Instead, your goal is to find a niche in pain and looking for a solution, then position your solution or new angle product in a way that makes it easy for them to buy.

2)   Research the competition

This is not to put you off, but to educate yourself as to what's already available, and of course to give you an idea if you could do better? It could also indicate where there is an opening for a new angle or approach on what's available, or something is missing from what is there already? You may have to *test-drive* the competitor's product, depending on what it is, and to see how you could improve upon it? Also, you could decide the particular niche is not worth your efforts?

Sometimes it is better to retreat than it is to push on!

3)   Create the product

The next thing is to start working on the product itself. Depending on what it is, you need to plan and get organised. I always believe in writing things down and keeping track of ideas, like I said. This is also where goal setting comes into play. Gather resources, develop a step-by-step process, concentrate your energy and frankly *get down to it*. If your product is an e-book, begin by writing a certain number of words per day, with certain corresponding chapters or sections. Just keep writing until it is finished, don't be worried about editing, etc, that comes later.

Quick Tip: Before you begin, and throughout the process, put your thoughts, ideas and inspiration down on a scratch-pad, jotter or notepad on your phone, etc. Just make sure you don't lose it? Those things can be worth gold.

----

4)   Create the sales funnel

You'll need a website and *email-capture* device. Your site will need good sales-copy (the words that sell your product). Don't always expect visitors to buy there and then, most people are inherently mistrusting initially, especially these days. This is why it's a good idea to have a reason for people to give you their email in exchange for free info or an informative report or something of **high perceived value**. In marketing, *no-list-means- no-money*, because you can't leverage the data. Once you have your list, you can regularly email your prospects (using an autoresponder), and build more of a closer relationship, which helps lubricate the wheels of decision.

5)   Develop your potential backend offers

Like I said, you want to offer multiple products to your front end buyers if you can, because it's one of the most effective ways to grow your income with an info-business. Once a person has made a purchase, and they are happy (*this is crucial*), they are more likely to buy from you again, if your backend meets their needs. Just remember, this is not about getting rich, it's about becoming free and comfortable. You can contact your front end buyers through email or mail with other synergistic offers.

There are obviously many nuances, distinctions and variables involved, but in a nutshell that's really all it takes. Clearly, the biggest part of the machine is finding the solution to people's pain and presenting your offer to them. Once you get your first product under your belt, your confidence and understanding grows exponentially.

If you create several income streams in your life, then you'll never have to worry about money again. Just ensure they are as passive and easy to manage as possible. It's pointless losing your freedom to the slavery of money. This book is all about escaping the mouse-wheel. You will need to have enough products *out-there* to generate the *release-money* you need in your journey away from obligation. You never know which product will be the one to hit the high sales, and which will flounder?

*It's the collective results of combined assets that
furnish your financial security.*

Just before we conclude this chapter, let's go back to selling a service for a second. One of the best ways I found to escape the 9-5 dive was through becoming a professional copywriter. See, I love to write and if you can earn being a writer, you're in heaven in my view. I started as a copywriter in the late 1990's, mostly a sideline income really. But then, it became more interesting and lucrative, so much so, often I would question the rationale behind other more labour intensive work I was doing and which was better to focus on? I enjoyed copywriting so much because you can get paid for what is simply writing words on a page. It's easy when you understand the process of copywriting. You won't be surprised to hear I created a product for it (copywriterbusiness.co.uk). Copywriting can beautifully dovetail with other products and money-making ideas you offer and can be part of a collective leap towards financial freedom. Plus it's a totally mobile business, which can be run from virtually anywhere in the world, via your Laptop.

At the end of the day, your info-business is about discovering where the pain is, then creating and promoting your solution. It's also about building *trust-based* relationships with people over a longer period. If you'd like more help getting started please visit:

www.ian-fox.com/financial-freedom

Power Tip:

1. Get to work finding a problem or pain people experience
2. Create the solution, then offer it
3. Build a recurring system

Fox Freedom Factor Maxim:

You are only one idea away from total financial freedom – so get thinking!

Chapter 13

Everything Comes To Those Who..?

If you said WAIT, then you are mistaken. Sometimes waiting is required, but mostly you have to act to make things happen. I used to tell my Martial Arts students, you won't achieve your Black Belt by waiting for it, or sitting on the couch munching potato chips! You've got to get down the Dojo and train. What you have to realise is selling information products online, or offline for that matter, is a gradual and sequential process. Look at making some extra money a week to start, then a few hundred a month. Followed by a few grand! It is possible and lots of people are already doing just that.

It's all about finding a trickle, then a stronger current, followed by a raging torrent. A lot of people get blinded by delusions of great wealth, and many buy into the patter of silk suited *"dream peddlers"* whose pitch consists of feeble wealth-building affirmations, whilst rubbing their big toe!

I have nothing against people taking training or mentoring; it's just that most so-called *"Gurus"* are false and pretentious. All they do is transfer their version of the world onto other people in the hope they will follow. Their mandate is conquer, consume and replace. Where money is a god!

There is a lot of hype around some people and they very much use the 'halo-effect' to boost their profile. But most are prisoners of their egos and sell the worn out illusion of success. All I ask you to do is recognise the truth from the BS! And watch who you listen to? Once you raise your consciousness about money and what freedom really means, your definition of "success" will change.

Learning and earning can be a challenge, especially when you have a knowledge deficit. But if everything were easy, nothing would be worth having. The truth is those who win money do not feel the same as those who earn it. The spiritual goal of your life is to rise above your circumstances whatever they are. Wherever you are in life, whatever your circumstances; this is where you begin the transformation taking place within you. Your destination is going beyond the mundane, but if mundane is what you experience then accept it fully, until such a time when change occurs. When the student is ready the teacher will appear!

To achieve anything you must take the *right action*. By right action I mean doing things which move you in the direction of your new-found freedom goals. There is a very fine line between strategic pushing and negative forcing, that few understand. We're trained from an early age, the more we force for our goals the better we'll feel, but no one's taught how to push in the right way or cope when things don't workout, which often happens.

Despite what I said earlier, occasionally you do need to bide your time when called for. What we perceive as loss, disappointment or failure is mostly wrapped up in the ego and expectations. Waiting can be a beautiful meditation that nurtures our soul.

105

Few people are good at waiting, and besides, you will never make a good decision when rushed, pushed, in fear or angry.

One of the biggest reasons people fail to become financially free is they get caught up in the major of minor things. Pushing in the wrong ways and at the wrong things. They lack self-belief and only try taking a few tentative actions which produce limited results. What you have to do is fully associate to what remaining trapped means to you and your family, and use this as a *driving force* to power you forward.

WHAT IS REALLY REQUIRED TO MOVE YOU FORWARD?

Stop thinking about winning and success; begin instead to concentrate on what is required to achieve the outcome you want. Look at the process of what's required, the steps, strategies, your strengths, your weakness and how you can develop these to your advantage.

I used to teach my students;

"You should not enter into battle unless your chance of victory is high, but equally you will not win the championship by fighting nobodies!"

Take measurable risks and accept calculated defeats. Light the fire in your belly and hone your skills to accept the challenges and take on the energy of a warrior. The more positive energy you give out, the more you get in return, so make sure you are focussing on what you want, not on what you don't. Life is a mirror image of your inner state and not the mask you wear for the outside world to see.

106

Be strong; be bold and think before you act. When your mind and body are talking the same language, your actions will speak your deepest intentions and deliver the best results for you. When you want to complete something you need *intention, concentration* and *action*, wrapped up in *patience* and *resilience*. Struggling to force things is not where you want to be placing your energy. If you hit a brick wall in something, you need to evaluate your choices and reactions. Not allowing the challenge to drag you into unconsciousness. If there is no way *around it, through it* or *over it*, then leave it for a while and evaluate your choices later on.

Don't turn your goal into martyrdom for a hollow cause. I realise in life you have to be determined and committed, but often the more you push something, the more you can push it away. Be aware of any unconscious reaction inside you, or if your ego is involved in the process. Everything comes to pass given time; but it's the ego that wants it now!

Realise too, you have an inner guide and trust in this part of your life. Spirit-guide, higher-self, God, call it whatever you want. It's an energy really, a feeling born out of a frequency. A connection to the divine, an omnipresent vibration, which is in the background of your life. It's more than a nice comforting feeling and more than the ego's way of trying to be special. It's around all of us, all the time. Those who are more connected to the vibration through spiritual practices such as meditation, prayer or Yoga, etc, feel it more than those whose level of existence is low frequency hum-drum.

You'll be in the right place at the right time because there is a part of you that has divine guidance, which becomes more active once you unblock and release the crud of your life. You don't have to struggle because this is always your choice!

By very nature of the current reality in which we live, life does have certain elements of limitation. We can't defy gravity or survive without oxygen, but have to accept these natural limits. Life is a place of learning how to overcome restriction and effort, and go beyond pedestrian to create your own reality. You are not here to be perfect, you are here to grow. Being and feeling free is eventually your destination, whilst living here on earth.

Power Tip:

1. Take concerted right action
2. The spiritual goal of your life is to rise above your circumstances whatever they are
3. Learn to foster the art of waiting

Fox Freedom Factor Maxim:

Align yourself to the inner guide that resides within you. The universal intelligence is part of who you are beyond thinking and opinions. Tap into this and your life will take on an expression of infinite possibilities

Chapter 14:

Bring More Lightness To Your Life

In Zen Buddhist teaching, it tells of the trees, which allow the birds to perch and fly away without either inviting them to stay or desiring them never to depart. In essence, if you become like the tree, your heart will be closer to the Tao, which is free. The more you attach yourself to things the more suffering you bring into your life. The more locked you are in consumerism and materialistic *object-consciousness*, the deeper your level of imprisonment. This is why getting rid of things is an essential meditation of your life. It affirms you are in control and not addicted to your stuff and possessions!

Chinese philosopher Lao Tzu, who wrote the Tao Te Ching, a philosophy about the Dao (or Tao); translated as the unseen mystical source of all existence, and the root of all things. Describes:

"In pursuit of knowledge, every day something is added. In the practice of the Tao, every day something is dropped. Less and less do you need to force things, until finally you arrive at non-action. When nothing is done, nothing is left undone. True mastery can be gained by letting things go their own way. It can't be gained by interfering."

This is why there is so much pain in the world. People *have* and *do* too much, *over* think, and their ego's *want* even more. The paradox is, for most people this is invisible, because they are caught up in the trance of everyday existence. They actually believe what they see, feel and experience is reality!

Many go against the natural state of things, against nature and the balance of harmony. Pushing against the current, fighting and arguing for the sake of it. Most of our society is laced with rules and rigidity. Your family and upbringing has engrained conditioned patterns in your mind. It can seem daunting to pull away from the *"norm"* and seek a different perspective, when everyone around you is materially and objective driven. But the only way to live in true freedom and to evolve is to extract yourself from the metaphorical umbilical cord of life's conditioning.

Humans parallel nature in their life-cycles and *in-out* rhythms. The Yin-Yang of human nature. You are born, grow, decay then die. That's the reality of life! The *"growth"* part of the equation is where most humans collect things such as experiences, possessions, associations, friends and enlarge their ego, reinforce their identity and increase their *consumer-lead, product–fed* minds. As time passes life gets ever intricate and complicated.

Then the whole function of life seems to be about reinforcing the identity of who you believe yourself to be? Whereas in nature, growth has a specific purpose and timeline, humans though keep pushing and are unable to stop. This is where most suffering and damage occurs.

Previously, if you wanted something and you couldn't afford it, would go out and get a loan, then think about paying for it later! The logic portion of your mind says, you can always pay it back, you'll be okay?! But then reality catches up and other unforeseen circumstances materialise. You have to pay the bare minimum to keep the tigers off your tail, as well as pay all your other obligations. The damn thing starts to stink up your life. One change of thought, a different question, a transmuted desire earlier on and life would now be so much different.

WEIGHT LOSS FOR THE SPIRIT

You can't change the past, but you can change what it meant and what you are going to do about the future. Make it your daily practice to *let something go*. Don't hold on to things. It could be a painful experience from the past or a recent argument or disproportioned reaction to those who you perceive to have offended you. Give up on keeping the emotional weight of things and bring more lightness into your life.

On a material level, sell the second car; give your designer labels to charity; give away the *un-needed* number of gadgets you have. Say goodbye to the crappy energy sapping friendships, saying, I wish you well. Everyday liberate yourself from the stuff you think makes up your life and your self-imposed identity. The more it hurts, the more healing the experience will be for you.

This will also reveal how much credence you have given to things that don't really matter?

As you do this, more and more junk will be cleared, and the more inner release you'll feel. You'll be back in *Yin*, which is soft, yielding, feminine and aware. Your eyes will open as you realise how much shit you have and how much crap it took to get it. You don't have to chuck everything out, just the things unworthy of the new you. Just make sure you don't keep something because your ego won't let you toss it? See beyond the object and imagine if you looked through time at the process which lead to you obtaining it in the first place. The amount of chemicals, materials used and the species that had to suffer because you wanted the darn object?

Success is about having less not having more.

This will be the new paradigm of the future, and many will have no other choice. When this happens, do not engage in futile resistance, but hone your spiritual resolve and commit to a lighter life.

Live your life outside the grip of the ego, consumed with object identification. Remember, you don't have to be perfect. You did not come here to be perfect, but to grow and learn. Most of our values of success stem from our parents and peers. Decide not to conform to what is nothing more than someone's idea of what your life should be. Step away from the rhythms of social and personal conditioning. This is another form of cutting loose of the things binding you to restriction and pain.

All things return to the dust from which they came eventually, nothing is permanent. Everything on the level of objects is ephemeral and decays. Things rust, age, and stop working, all forming part of the wear and tear written into the contract of humanity.

Objects get replaced with new shiny buttons and faster speeds. Society brainwashes us into believing we need new things and frowns upon us if what we have is old and out of fashion!

You will get old, you will decay and you will die. This is one of the reasons you need to become free and liberated from your possessions as quickly as you can. The last thing you need is to learn this lesson when you're too crusty to do anything about it. When people become too attached to their identity and lifestyle, there is a great deal of resistance once these things change. *The "in" rhythm returns.* The inability to adapt to the changing rhythms of life is one of the mental afflictions of most people. It causes untold suffering and anguish. But, when you master your reality, perception and ego, you transcend the low-level energy and rise to a much higher frequency.

You become more transparent in your everyday existence. You are not hiding behind opinions, status symbols and designer clothes. Your thoughts become more inclusive and you are more *we* than "me!" You don't see yourself a separate entity any longer, struggling to survive, trying to become someone, paving the way for your ego to control, collect and conquer.

THE MOST POWERFUL MANTRA EVER WRITTEN

You become one with all things. *'Unity, Peace and Harmony'* become your ultimate mantra. No matter what you have done up to this point, tomorrow is a new sunrise and a chance for you to change. A few years from now an empty space will mark the spot where you once stood. *This is why now is your time to change.*

Power Tip:

1. You can't change the past, but you can change what it meant
2. Everyday give something away
3. Success is about having less not having more

Fox Freedom Factor Maxim:

Adapt yourself to the rhythms of life. Don't hold on to things and surrender to the inevitable

Chapter 15:

The Fear Solution

I touched on this earlier, but it's so important, worth covering in-depth again, because left unchecked and not eliminated, will stagnate any chances you have to being truly free.

Fear is the biggest killer of your freedom and liberation.

Here I will offer you some additional tools to help you recognise, remove and replace the crushing energy that fear creates. We live in fearful times *(when have we not?)*. People fear for their job, pensions, security and many, the very fabric of their lives. They sense change and the ego doesn't like that, because it craves certainty in it's never ending quest to be given stimulus and fed sensory pleasure. The greatest fear and challenge is letting go of objects and thought-forms in your life.

One of your toughest obstacles is controlling your emotions and thoughts during *'testing'* times and tackling any deep-seated fears holding you back from becoming free. When I teach fighters how to overcome fight fear and nerves, I say to them; to combat fear you have to understand and control two things; *Psychology* and *Physiology*.

Many a 'would be' great fighter has lost, because they were not mentally prepared and ready to take the fight. It doesn't matter whether you're fighting an opponent externally or yourself internally, fear has to be handled in the same way. It's just a different set of circumstances.

Many fears are deep rooted and are not easily detected, but as you become more conscious those hidden emotions may come to the surface before they are finally released. I'm sure you've been in situations where fear and nerves got the better of your performance and outcome? It's normal to have feelings about going into battle or doing something uncomfortable, because it's not natural to have someone trying to hurt you, or your ego weakened.

The main problem is when those feelings and emotions become out of control or counter productive to your desired outcome. The fear emotion is a protective device which can serve a positive purpose. If fear stops you from risking potential injury or a life threatening situation, then in that instance, fear is a good thing.

The problem is when fear keeps you trapped and enclosed in a small and rarefied atmosphere. Encasing you in an illusionary bubble of security. Governments, advertisers, the news, friends and family all use fear in various guises to elicit a desired response or outcome. Quite often they are not conscious of what they are doing. If you don't do this, then this will happen. Do this or else! Fear is the ultimate motivator of 'the people' and single greatest enemy of your freedom. It is not what we can or can't accomplish, but the fears we have, holding us back from breaking through the barriers of self limitation. Fear is the illusionary game we play to limit our efforts and accept the card deck of life.

Some say they have no fear, but to have fear is human, and to overcome is divine! Growth is having peace and the *Great Spirit* in your heart. It's about having the courage to go from a materially driven object filled life to becoming a more minimalist being, no longer afraid of transformation.

You embrace *Small Wants and have Little Needs*. You refute the showy self and value the infinite power of the inner world. Essentially, you return to nature and Yin.

Conquering fear is also about willing to become invisible at times. By that, I mean not looking for people to observe, accept or notice you. Remaining in the shadows and holding back for the urge to charge at the front line. Pushing your chest out and thrusting your hips at life makes the statement you are insecure and seeking admirers to fill the empty void you feel inside. It's a way of masking the hidden fears clutching at your heart. You have to be prepared to be *"imperfect."* Keep back. Stay in control. Don't react. Keep quiet. Catch yourself in the act of wanting to show off or boost your ego, and STOP!

Refrain from trivial banter or the pressure of putting what you had for dinner on your social networking pages. Don't say a word!

Ask yourself:

"What is my authentic intention?" in all situations.

There are many elements to fear, but most are wrapped around some form of perceived or actual loss. With Martial Arts tournaments, its pre fight anxiety and fight day jitters. With life, it could be loss of a job, a material object, a situation or the thought of losing something now or in the future.

117

The ego does not like to lose and the mind creates the fertile ground on which imaginary fears, doubts and worries can be cultivated. When you think about it, very few fears are real. A small element of perception can grow into an emotional rollercoaster, standing on the foundations of inaccuracies and misjudgements. Few things are ever as they appear to be. Your perception creates your reality.

The main problem with fear and anxiety is it builds up slowly, where people go inside and make pictures of terrible outcomes and repeat them over and over. They become their own worst enemy, and then wonder why life turns to crap? Most fears are disproportionate to the event or potential outcome. What you are afraid of is not what you think, in as much as a person who fears heights is not afraid of the height itself.

SEE FEAR AS A FRIEND WHO HAS OUTSTAYED THEIR WELCOME

The first step to overcoming fear is to identify what you are really afraid of? It's the way the brain processes information and how it represents facts. Not everyone is afraid of heights or every fighter afraid of fighting. When you break things down you'll recognise the illusionary components all fears contain. You'll also see how the ego and the fear are inextricably intertwined. When you identify what you are really afraid of, you will see it for what it actually is, *truth will reveal itself*, and how it appears to the mind.

This revelation will completely transform your feelings and emotions, and at some level you may see the fear as a friend who has outstayed their welcome. For many people there is a secondary gain to their fears.

118

When fear arises you need to channel those emotions into positive outcomes which support your desires. Ultimately fear cannot exist in the present, because its life depends on living in the past or projecting itself into the future. When you focus on the step you are taking right now, fear finds it difficult to exist. So, if you are worried about paying debts or which product you are going to start, instead concentrate your energy on the present step you need to take, not the daunting end result.

If you are afraid or stressed about something, this is a sign your ego is activated and a signal you need to take stock, pull back and focus on the current thing you need to do. Having courage to recognise and work on your fears is a big step in your definitive evolution. When you face things and accept where you are emotionally, you transcend to a higher dimension, far beyond normal humans, who plod on pushing against the current tide along with the rest of the multitudes.

By facing up to things, you have at your disposal, a great opening for incredible awareness and growth.

You send out a powerful affirmation; *you are more than your circumstances and life conditions.* You become responsible for your emotions and accept you are the cause of your fears at a core level. Look at fear as an opening gateway. At first you need some force to commence the opening, but then as you remove the layers of compacted emotion, the perspective of the swing becomes wider.

You must work through your fears. Remember, the things you feel are the result of psychological and chemical processes taking place in your mind and body. Just try to put things into a *thought-form* which supports you.

119

Although it is a cliché, it is nevertheless true; *the only thing to fear is fear itself.* Fear is a gateway opening before you, step forward and be free!

The weight of engrained, conditioned fear patterns dissolve the moment you agree to let go. A new beginning will emerge in your life, drawing you to a new destiny. As long as your decision to break away from fear is real and genuine, beyond a fleeting whim. You turn away from apprehensions, the dread, the trepidation, and you become a fearless warrior.

In a way, you must train the mind for combating and facing what you fear. This doesn't always mean taking up skydiving because you fear heights. The destructive fears I'm referring to are those holding you back from becoming free in this life. Fearing to take action, fearing to letting go, to moving on, etc. I would always suggest to my Martial Arts students that along with your physical training, put yourself mentally in the ring, cage or on the mat and fully associate with the noises, the crowd, the sweat, the anxiety, the other guy's corner – *what ever it takes to be there fully.*

Rehearse the fight in your head. Think about being afraid, but then imagine, you're at the movies and you are acting out the scene on the screen, only float out of your body and sit in the audience watching yourself acting out the fear on the screen. Once the movie has stopped, run it backwards to the beginning and start watching it again. Now float out of your body, which is sitting in the chair, and go to the balcony looking at yourself sitting in the chair watching yourself in the movie. Then run the movie backwards and start watching it again. Now as the third person on the balcony, looking back at yourself in the chair and on the screen being afraid, I want you to say in a stern voice *"my fear is totally stupid."*

As you look at yourself being afraid, whilst watching yourself being afraid, something inside you will feel very different about the situation. This worked wonders for Martial Arts, and is quite amazing for other things too. *Just make the move and do it!*

Over the years I have taught *firewalking* seminars and *Extreme Personal Development* techniques. These include board breaking Karate style, breaking an arrow in the throat, and more powerful exercises, such as bending a re-bar (concrete reinforcement bar) between two people placed in the throat, and also driving a 5 inch needle through the hand. These are not performed to attest how macho you are, but represent a potent metaphor for recognising and eliminating personal fears and limiting beliefs.

In essence, the techniques are relatively easy; the challenge is the psychological fortitude required and overcoming the fear pushing you back. This is a parallel I draw to life, where by most things are easy; it's the mental side making it appear difficult. Some people actually manifest struggle through their fearful thought projections.

THE NEEDLE THROUGH THE HAND

Out of all the things I have taught, the 5-inch needle *through the hand* represents the greatest barrier for most people. Many would go white as a sheet just watching the process; others would feel sick and make a 360° turn for the exit. It's easy to see who had the most intense internal barriers, just watching the thing, whilst not actually doing it. It's the same in life, people are afraid of things they have not even attempted!

When trained, there is no pain or blood doing the needle. It creates a state of pure clarity, bliss and mental freedom. It's used to empower you through the process of the seemingly impossible. It releases a level of awareness few will ever experience and understand. Try being afraid after that! It can crush anxiety, demolish depression, and dispel many other mental and physical conditions in a snap! How do I know? Because I've used it as a healing tool with clients.

I use the acronym **"F.A.C.E. I.T."** to describe each of the necessary steps you should do to handle Fear.

F – Facts. Get factual about what you are really afraid of. See fear as it really is, not how your mind manipulates reality. Fears are often implanted by parents, friends, politicians and advertisers, etc; because they know fear is very persuasive. There could also be disproportionate associations and reactions to earlier life experiences. The more awake you are when someone attempts to implant a fear, the more you will question the content of the information and decipher the real facts. Then perhaps even reject the idea before it grows.

A – Action. Do something about your fear and anxiety. Fear hates motion. The more you move the less you fear. The emotion of fear is like a bubble of energy, once you penetrate the initial layer; you see things from a different perspective and position. Deep breathe, move your body, and progress towards your fear, not away, (provided there is no physical danger of course).

C – Confidence. Get confident about your ability. Having said that, make sure you have the tools to complete the job? Build up your personal power by taking smaller steps towards conquering your fear. Break the fear down into small manageable chunks and attack one section at a time. If heights "*were*" your problem, practice these techniques, and safely climb a few feet higher than you're used to, then move back, and go a bit higher next time. Small steps become giant leaps eventually. Your confidence grows and your sphere of influence expands.

E – Evolve. Rise above your fears and emotions; see them as teachers, guides and gateways. It's delusional to think you can evolve out of your current circumstances without recognising and eliminating your fears. Expecting things to miraculously change in the future, where you will be free and liberated will never happen unless you *actively work on yourself.* Until you work on self-growth, you will always fall deeper into unconsciousness.

You instantly evolve the moment you become more aware of yourself and the fears you hold in your heart. You experience an incredible realisation, which as previously mentioned, you do indeed create your own reality. People who are free, do the things and take the actions those who remain trapped would never do!

Transcend fear and the world will be yours.

I – Information. Gather as much information as you can about your fear. Don't use content to disempower you, but view things in a detached way, so you can gather the information on the **F**alse **E**vidence **A**ppearing to be **R**eal of it all. More or less everyone has heard this acronym before and some say it's become a cliché? But how many *intellectually* know it, but do not use and live by it?

I said it earlier; *knowledge dispels fear*, the more you understand, the less you are afraid. The other way to look at it, is bombard your fear with all the new distinctions and resources you have garnered from this book.

T – Test. One of the most powerful ways to overcome something is to actually confront it head-on, if safe to do so. Test how you handle fear by taking on smaller less prominent ones, such as going on scary rides, talking to people in situations where you lack confidence, doing smaller things you fear and overcoming them. This will build a *body-of-belief* inside you, becoming a powerhouse of stored experience you can tap into when it really matters. Your mind and body become a reference point, depicting a life of courageous acts.

TAKE CONTROL

Your outward manifestation is purely the result of your inward expression of where you are in your mind, ego, beliefs and spirituality. Life will have challenged you and trampled on your dreams no doubt. But the one thing you always have control over is how you react to anything that happens to you. No one can take this way.

Being more *flexible* and *adaptable* is key to a healthy mind and body. When you are afraid of something, don't try to resist it or create a *"personal story"* out of it. This just reinforces the fear and compounds the stress it causes. Seek the harmonious path and align with your authentic powers and infinite wisdom.

ACTION KILLS FEAR, AVOIDANCE REINFORCES IT

So, in essence you have to break through the bubble and recognise, remove and replace the illusionary fears dwelling in your heart. Overcoming fears or negative emotions needs constant attention over time, it's like building muscle, grows stronger with repetition.

Action kills fear, avoidance reinforces it. There will come a point in your life when you are no longer afraid, but why wait, when the gateway is always just before you and ready for you to open.

Have the courage to step forward. Go on I dare you!

"Courage is being scared to death and saddling up anyway."
John Wayne.

Power Tip:

1. When afraid **F.A.C.E. I.T.**
2. When fear arises you need to channel those emotions into positive outcomes, which support your desires
3. You create your own reality

Fox Freedom Factor Maxim:

Don't let your life be a warning but a message of hope, certainty and authentic reality

Chapter 16

Mission Freedom

The final chapter of this book is about putting it all together, and making the journey from *slavery to freedom* and from ego to *raising your spiritual consciousness*, and calling freedom into your life. I know it's been tough for you. It's been challenging, and pushed some buttons no doubt. The journey is never easy, nor is it always pleasant, but it *MUST* happen. Perhaps the unconsciousness in you has been stirred by the consciousness inside this book?

I don't really know where you are in your level of consciousness? But the human condition is one of perpetual disappointment, yearning, reaction, problem creation, fear and feelings of inadequacy. That is of course, until you raise your consciousness beyond the realm of compulsive thinking, form identification and ego.

Your life is ultimately about embarking on a spiritual journey of *joyful* freedom. I use the word *joyful*, because many people get lost in the egoic pursuit of freedom and experience little ego –free *joy* in their lives, along the way. Joy does not come from enjoying material pleasures, because these are fleeting and more often reinforce the ego. Things come and go, and what brings you pleasure now ultimately fades away eventually.

This does not mean you can't appreciate certain earthly pleasures, because many can have a beneficial spiritual component. You can have your *"nice"* things, dandy clothes and the big house, if you really want them? The question to ask yourself at any point is this: *"is all this feeding my ego?"*

YOUR SPIRITUALITY IS THE ONLY THING THAT REALLY MATTERS

Are you deriving your personal identity from these *things*? Do you use *things* and people to help elevate your perception of self? Essentially your life's mission is to transcend the ego and energise your spirit. Because your level of *spirituality is the only thing that really matters*. This is what the journey of life is all about. When you begin to transcend the ego and its alluring illusions, you open up inside an incredible all pervading energy. Call it Christ consciousness, the Buddha, or Pure White Light, or any name you wish, the nametag is not important.

The truth is, you are raising your energy and consciousness, not to be more attractive and powerful or to make loads of cash, but to open your heart and mind to a new found freedom and to become more than your current existence. With this, you will make what you need to elevate your way out of current circumstances and move closer to your destiny. You appreciate most people are slaves, held hostage by their egos and consume far more than they will ever need. They rush around from one drama and crisis to another, trying to make sense of it all! This has probably been a close description of your life at times?

On the other hand, you will live your life through alert attention, rather than reactive impulsion. You are very aware of your ego, and when it's sliding into unconscious thinking. You emit a light into this world that becomes a beacon of hope.

If your life could be represented as a Flute, then your thoughts should be the breath, which produces beautiful serene music, echoing in your heart, not some screechy racket, resembling two cats fighting on a tin roof.

Part of this experience is evolving out of the strengthening and conditioning of your ego, which some call the *ego-death*. This will be the hardest part for you, because resistance can be fierce. You'll experience glimpses of *ego-death*, and in that moment, see life totally differently. It will be as though you've just awakened from a long sleep or deep trance.

YOU DON'T NEED AS MUCH MONEY AS YOU THINK TO BE FREE

In reality, more than having a lot of money and material wealth, other things become more important and valuable. Truth is you don't need as much money as you think to be free. Feeling safe, being comfortable, freedom of choice, an easy pace of life, and living in peace, *all have incredible value over having more money*. The other powerful thing to help you on your way is to become more passive (*conscious*), when stressful and reactive situations occur.

As you begin to evolve and grow out of your ego state, you will feel uncomfortable at times; because the ego is clinging to life. Some feel as though their lives are falling apart. It's at that point you have an epiphany, because you break away from the lifelong grip of the ego and ascend above the life you once knew. It's an incredible portal and opportunity.

As the process unfolds, another part of your ego falls away, revealing your true spiritual self. You raise your energy and heighten your perceptions. But you will be challenged along the way; it's not called the spiritual path for nothing. I call it the *Spiritual Hill*. Growth is not always easy, but neither is staying the same and is potentially far worse. When conscious, you are aware you are growing and aware of how to respond in all circumstances.

EVERYTHING THAT HAPPENS TO YOU IS ANOTHER OPPORTUNITY TO AWAKEN

Without diving into every difficult situation you can find, or willing more pain into your life, allow yourself to be challenged, because you know you will grow. You accept you are work in progress. Experience is a frame of reference you can draw upon when needed in the future and acts as a roadmap to a calmer more tranquil life. When you are on this path, everything that happens to you is another opportunity to awaken. It's all about paying close attention to what is going on and what you are feeling moment to moment, because *life is a feeling!* There is always someone trying to press their ideas, thoughts and attitudes on you and many live their entire lives in a constant state of reaction and opposition. But this is *NOT* your destiny, is it?

I used to tell my students, *"Fake it then make it."* This would apply to being more self confident, self assured or practising a technique they'd never tried before. Rather than simply thinking how difficult it was or reciting negative self talk. Just pretend you know it, until you *know it!* You can use the same thing next time you're anxious about money. Imagine you're abundant and trust you will be ok.

This is not cuckoo-crap, but a shift in your energy and perception. You'll still need to take action where applicable though. You seldom trip over change. When your consciousness moves away from the mainstream fears and anxieties of the masses, you'll feel more inner peace and relief.

Speaking of money again, to ultimately be free you need enough money to sustain yourself and having money also comes down to your self-worth. If you think you'll always be poor and broke, then essentially this is what you create. Believing other people have better chances and opportunities than you is just a conditioned pattern you've been running inside your mind. It's been strengthened over time through repetition. You've sucked up the pain of negative experience and bought into the bullshit mandate of scarcity. By disengaging the ego and pushing through fear you open yourself to life's offerings.

YOU ARE WORTHY

Tell yourself *"I am worthy"* on a regular basis, but when you do, just make sure you're not just trying to fuel the ego. It's not about telling yourself, *"I am worthy of this new BMW!"* With its 60 months of slavery and obligation. BMW is an acronym for *'Blow My Wad,'* wad of money! When you open your heart and raise your consciousness, you will be putting out the right frequency and understand the difference between being spiritually abundant and egoically bankrupt.

It's making certain your outer purpose (Yang) is not eclipsing your inner purpose (Yin). Having money just to appear to be *"special"* is a waste of time and life, if your spirituality is a barren wasteland.

Overcoming your attachment to outcome and objects, but still feeling in your heart you are worthy of receiving is the balancing condition you have to constantly work on. When lack of abundance thinking occupies the mind, insecurity and scarcity consciousness takes over, and a state of perpetual fear becomes the background hum of your life. Accept though, sometimes spiritual progress is snail pace slow. Yang (ego-forcing), is fast whereas Yin (natural flow), is easy-going.

Make Yin your regular practice, then your energy will raise and you'll realise "*it*" (stuff, things, situations, etc) won't matter so much anymore. The shift happens when the time is right! When the inner and outer you is in synergy.

The banks, big businesses, and the media all push Yang at people, like it was the only thing which mattered. Corrupting our children, brainwashing the people, encasing them in a trance of slavery and debt. The evil, pain and suffering caused by the worship of green paper! This is slave behaviour in its many manifestations! It has to, and WILL stop. This is the other reason you need to change the circumstances and conditions of your life.

OPEN YOUR HEART

You must be part of the solution, not join the collective unconscious cascading to the edge of the cliff. An end to the old you, a birth to the new you, and the initiation of your sacred personal awakening. In the end, the gateway to eternal freedom is how big your heart was, not your ego. You can only be eternally remembered for that.

HELP PEOPLE AND THE MONEY WILL COME

If you are reading this book because your only reason is to earn money or become wealthy and *"secure,"* then you're missing the real point. That is the illusion of Yang, fed to you by the power hungry megalomaniacs of our society. Money and security are by products of your level of energy, consciousness and self awareness. When you align to your higher purpose and help people, the money will come.

THE COLLECTIVE INSANITY

Those who chase money purely for the sake of it or the collective insane on a giant power-trip will implode eventually. Sometimes leading to tragic consequences, such as the insanity perpetrated by UK businessman Christopher Foster, who murdered his wife, daughter and animals because his ego couldn't cope with a change in financial circumstances? The full horror of this case shocked even the most hardened police and fire investigators. There are plenty of other situations similar to this one, perhaps not as severe, but nevertheless causing suffering to others. No doubt as you read this, many more people and animals are suffering because of the madness of the ego. What you have to remember is the majority of the planet when unconscious, lives in constant fear or unease to a greater or lesser degree.

Your purpose is to shine a light on the darkness of the world, by helping heal pain.

Worry and anxiety about money only serve to propel you faster on the conveyer belt of pessimism and destruction, pulling the feelings, circumstances and states you most want to avoid.

Besides, I've already said money alone will never bring security, because security is always a state of consciousness. By healing and loving yourself, you open up to a level of freedom that no amount of money could buy.

This is certainly a way for you to escape the rat-race, and synthetic, vacuum-packed, shrink-wrapped society we live in. You can start living authentically without the bondage of conformity of egoic entrapment. You are not a slave to your job or circumstances, but a spiritual freedom fighter on a quest for change, and if you do things right you'll have lots of it (*change*) in your pocket!

This is a book you *DO*, not one you start and never finish, or only read once, then leave to vanish into the fog of an over cluttered book shelf built on the foundations of good intentions. You see, that's what separates the enlightened from the collective unconscious, those who are controlled and influenced by the media and daily news, which is sadly most people. What you are predominantly subjected to becomes your distorted view of reality. The slave-trade programming of the unconsciousness of the ego.

SEE EVERYTHING AS A SPIRITUAL PORTAL

You are looking to activate an arising consciousness and create a spiritual perspective of life and all things. A spiritual being is who you *truly* are beyond your name, identity, and how much you have in the bank. When internal re-alignment occurs, many feel as though they are remembering where they came from and who they are beyond the modern electronically stimulated culture in which we live.

Ancient humanity's power has been misplaced in a world obsessed with money, status and glamour. However, things are changing because the soul of the planet is in transition. As your energy expands you will *grow*, not suffer, and look at life as a spiritual doorway or portal. Always read between the lines of your perceived experience. Therein rests the hidden message coded by God, deciphered by your consciousness and revealed in your understanding.

WHAT'S YOUR STRAWBERRY?

A Zen monk walking across a field was chased by a tiger. He ran as fast as his little legs would carry him. He came to the edge of a steep cliff, catching hold of a vine; he lowered himself over the edge to escape the gnashing jaws. Feeling reprieved he looked down in shock to see another tiger waiting below him. Then in a weird turn of fate, two mice appear from a hole in the cliff and begin eating the vine.

Whilst contemplating his predicament, the monk notices a juicy fat strawberry poking out of a lush plant near to him. Placing it inside his dry mouth, the vine eventually snaps and he falls to his death. On the way to certain earthly departure at the claws and jaws of the tiger, he gives total commitment to the sweet taste of the strawberry.

There will always be situations and circumstances where tigers will chase you. *You must make it your sacred purpose to always see the strawberry!* If financial or any circumstances for that matter, are tough, look for the sweet strawberry, don't choose to suffer the tigers around you. Invariably choose consciousness over suffering. The ultimate truth of life is you *create your own reality*. You decide on how much joy or pain you wish to create in the development of your consciousness. Rich, poor, happy, sad – it's only ever about how conscious you are. When your consciousness is expanded nothing can touch you, no matter how deep the tiger's claws penetrate.

SEE MONEY AS ENERGY

More than cash in the bank, being free is in direct proportion to your inner knowledge, having the right kind of information and encompassing the highest perception and awareness of your life. Being able to perceive the truth of things and having an acute sense of where your thoughts, mind and energy is being directed is critical to living in freedom.

Once aligned you'll know when something feels right.

Perception and energy will allow you to connect with the right circumstances and people. Money is energy in every sense of the word, which can only ever buy experience. Thoughts have a high vibrational frequency that will transport abundance and freedom to you, once the ego is subjugated. I know I've already said it, but worth mentioning again because repetition leads to recognition. Forget trying to be special or perfect or looking for people to observe you. It's the delusion of the masses and balances precariously on the hinges of self-destruction.

Being recognised means there will come a point when you are no longer recognised. The pendulum swings the other way, as it were. Things have their creation, lifespan, decay and decrease structure. People use others like a scaffold that supports their need to feel important and separate from everyone else. They think being noticed makes them more alive, more special. In the end it only serves to highlight their dysfunction and pain.

The Buddha said, *"A wise man, recognising that the world is but an illusion, does not act as if it is real, so he escapes suffering."*

For many, life is the illusion of an heroic struggle. They live in constant pain and confusion, the unknown scares them and they lack certainty about the future. But it does not have to be this way, even if those tigers are at your heels. You do have a choice. The legacy of the planet does not have to be one of suffering. More importantly, your life does not have to be a struggle. This is what this book is all about. That's why I wrote it and why it's vital you not only read, but follow and act on it as well.

Don't just sit there intellectualising the words on the page.

Take Action...

...on what you read and become more than your current situation and perception. Practice having *Small Wants and Little Needs* in your life, starting today.

To be free means the extinction of the obsessive, materially self-driven ego which obscures reality and presents many illusions as real-life. This is what I referred to earlier as the *ego-death*. Not easy to achieve, especially when the ego is strong and dominant. When you see yourself as part of *all* things and not as a separate entity, you disengage from the roots of your ego driven mind and experience a new, much richer level of freedom in your life. You have to become more intuitive and seek something more powerful and real, than the bankrupt illusion of success or being rich and famous.

Disengage your mind from the trap of overt materialism and you will evoke a higher dimensional frequency of spirituality and awareness. Your eyes will open to an otherwise invisible reality. Huge change is coming to the forefront of mankind. Just look at how much change there has been over the last few years, of which there is more to come! This book is in your hand for a reason, beyond making a few extra notes a month. Perhaps you've been inwardly guided or felt drawn to it, because deep in your heart you know you want change, and the pulse of human evolution is beating stronger.

LIFE IS A MIRROR

You are not your programming, conditioning or family, but an individual who is reaching their highest potential and spiritual intensity, beyond being a number or "stat" to the deities of consumerism. Life is a mirror reflecting back to you what you put out, and is a precise gauge of where you are spiritually and emotionally. So, money in and of itself will not release you, if you are emotionally hung-up, judgmental, vindictive and self-centred.

You can be happier now, living in a one bedroom apartment than a person in a ten bedroom mansion. It's all relative to your state of mind and perceived consciousness. Besides, you can only ever be in one room at a time and only ever sit in one chair, and think of all the dusting that needed doing, the maintenance and heating costs, just to make yourself feel special. It's not worth it!

When you're on a spiritual quest there is no finish line. It's much like peeling an onion, when one layer is removed another one appears. On an ego level it would be nice to feel as though you'd finished. Made it to utopia as it were, and your life is finally complete. But growth and consciousness is a continual evolving process. Like studying the Martial Arts, you can never know enough or should I say, become conscious enough to know you really don't know anything!

STEP AWAY FROM GLAMOUR AND LIFE'S MERRY GO-ROUND OF ILLUSIONS

I guess if you owe little, have money in the bank and are not shackled to the timeline of someone else's plan, or a self-employed workaholic, then you can safely say, you are more free than most. But I feel because you are reading this, you are looking for a spiritual and practical leg-up. The truth is this; you have to *step away from the glamour and incessant merry go-round of illusions* out there, being churned out by the media and unconscious friends and family. In the end, spirit will always trump status and wealth, because once genuinely gained can never be lost, whereas money comes and goes, hence the term *currency*. Spirituality is all pervading and evolving, eventually eclipsing earthly wants and desires.

You must have the courage to see beyond today, and the self awareness to wake up from the trance, to see the bankrupt system for what it is. It's time to heal yourself and the planet and get out of the *rat-race*.

All you need to do is three things;

1: Decide what you want to do?
2: Create a plan of action
3: Follow the plan until actualized

Yes, I know the devil is in the details, but simplicity is my way, not making things more complicated than they need to be. Your life evolves the moment you make a powerful and conscious decision about where you want it to go. Look at your day-to-day situations, stresses and struggles as portals to opportunity and enlightenment. *See the truth for what it is*. It's the decisions you make about where you want to be and what you want to do, which sets your life apart from that of the herd.

Welcome change into your life, and bring *fearlessness and resourcefulness* into any circumstance, no matter what form or shape they take. You then become the master of your own universe and the architect of change. You get nearer and clearer in your mind and body to what you want for your life, when you let go of the crud. You start to create pure clarity.

IT'S YOUR BIRTH RIGHT TO BE FREE

As you align to your new freedom and consciousness you'll feel completely alive, calm and resolute. You have unshakeable inner strength, and you'll attract good things towards you, because you are more serene, balanced and focused.

So, your daily task is to break away from ego, get rid of things, consume less, and love more. Release yourself from the *"story"* and *"content"* of your life, your history, past mistakes and negative beliefs and thoughts. It's your birth right to be free, not continue locked in a box of conformity and control. Let go of the need to feed your ego, don't become its slave by purchasing more stuff and living off debt. Become more aware of the space before your mind reacts to stimulus and outside influence. Then you'll be on your way to complete freedom, deep inner joy, and live in total peace.

Accept who you are, where you find yourself now, and energize your life with purposeful intention and right action. Believe you can do it no matter what happens, or what other people say. *Move your attention, intention and energy towards being spiritually and financially free.*

It's not just about having more money, it's about having **'Small Wants and Little Needs'** and feeling greater happiness and joy regardless of status and possessions, which invariably pollute your life and clog the arteries of mother earth. If in writing this book you're stirred to move and change your life, then my time has been more than worth it. You owe it to yourself to escape the brainwashing, manipulations and nefarious influences of unconscious individuals. It's your time to stand up and shine through the darkness.

It's also creating those exquisite experiences and enjoying the beauty of this planet. It's about living with love and joy in your heart every moment and having a conscious choice about how you live your life. Create your own destiny from this point on. Look the world in the eye and affirm this is it, the time is now, and I am ready.

"Our deepest fear is not that we are inadequate. Our deepest fear beyond measure is that we are powerful beyond measure. It is our light not darkness that frightens us most." Nelson Mandela

ABOUT THE AUTHOR

Ian Fox is a spiritual visionary who's helped thousands of people worldwide with his unique, down-to-earth and highly experiential approach to self-awareness and spirituality. A renowned Martial Arts Master and mind and body teacher with over 35 years experience. Founder of the Ian Fox Wellbeing System, a holistic training company, which has trained over 6000 instructors globally since 1994.

Ian has taught Extreme Personal Development for many years as a powerful and transformational method for overcoming fear and achieving higher spiritual consciousness. He is also a Reiki and Sekhem master and specialises in Dynamic Healing, a fusion of practical energy techniques, transformational healing mantras, language patterns and empowering rituals. Ian teaches mind and body empowerment and 'real-world' spirituality ensuring powerful and lasting results. He's appeared on Television programmes, in magazines and on Radio all over the world.

Ian grew up in poverty, being one of 10 children, and after many years of struggle, his intention was not only to become financially free, but more spiritually conscious at the same time. He's attained spiritual and financial freedom and now wants to share his epiphany, insights and secrets with the readers of this book. Ian believes every human being can live spiritually and financially free now, and give back to humanity.

For more information about books, courses, seminars and products by Ian Fox please visit: www.ian-fox.com or www.ianfoxwellbeingsystem.com